What They Say About Us

"One organization with a long record of success in helping people find jobs is The Five O'Clock Club."
FORTUNE

"The Five O'Clock Club's arrival in D.C. reflects the growing importance of . . . career development."
The Washington Post

"Many managers left to fend for themselves are turning to the camaraderie offered by [The Five O'Clock Club]. Members share tips and advice, and hear experts."
The Wall Street Journal

"If you have been out of work for some time . . . consider The Five O'Clock Club."
The New York Times

"Wendleton has reinvented the historic gentlemen's fraternal oasis and built it into a chain of strategy clubs for job seekers."
The Philadelphia Inquirer

"Organizations such as The Five O'Clock Club are building . . . an extended professional family."
Jessica Lipnack, author, *Professional Teams*

"[The Five O'Clock Club] will ask not what you do, but 'What do you want to do?' . . . [And] don't expect to get any great happy hour drink specials at this joint. The two-hour seminars are all business."
The Washington Times

"The Five O'Clock Club's proven philosophy is that job hunting is a learned skill like any other. The Five O'Clock Club becomes the engine that drives [your] search."
Black Enterprise

"Job hunting is a science at The Five O'Clock Club. [Members] find the discipline, direction and much-needed support that keeps a job search on track."
Modern Maturity

"Wendleton tells you how to beat the odds—even in an economy where pink slips are more common than perks. Her savvy and practical guide[s] are chockablock with sample résumés, cover letters, worksheets, negotiating tips, networking suggestions and inspirational quotes from such far-flung achievers as Abraham Lincoln, Malcolm Forbes and Lily Tomlin."
Working Woman

"On behalf of eight million New Yorkers, I commend and thank The Five O'Clock Club. Keep the faith and keep America working!"
David N. Dinkins, former Mayor,
The City of New York

"Kate Wendleton has written a sage and sensible book for the turbulent 90's."
Harvey Mackay, author of *Swim with the Sharks Without Being Eaten Alive*

"Everyone who has met Kate knows that she has a genius for caring about others."
David Rottman, vice president and manager, Career Services,
Chase Manhattan Bank, New York City

"During the time I was looking for a job I kept Kate's books by my bed. I read a little every night, a little every morning. Her common-sense advice, methodical approach, and hints for keeping the spirits up were extremely useful."
    Harold Levine, coordinator, Yale Alumni Career Resource Network

"Everyone talks about 'taking charge' of their lives; Kate Wendleton shows you how. One of the savviest and most effective career counselors that I know teaches that—even in the toughest of times—you can (and deserve to) find work that is right for you."
    Robert Mintz, director of Human Resources, Time, Inc., Magazines

"Today's job market is the toughest I've seen, and it requires the combination Kate has struck: shrewdness about the hiring process and the courage to face inner issues. Great work!"
    William Pilder, chairman, TransKey

"Kate Wendleton offers a wealth of pragmatic, uplifting advice for the job seeker. A person who follows Kate's formula would certainly get my attention, even if I'd already rejected his or her résumé."
    Carole F. St. Mark, president,
    Pitney Bowes Logistics Systems & Business Services

"Kate breaks the process into doable steps that are easy to understand."
    Albert Prendergast, senior vice president, Human Resources, Mastercard International

"A one-woman crusade against unemployment—Kate Wendleton and The Five O'Clock Club!"
    Roberta Mell,
    vice president, National Advertising, Home Box Office

"Kate is one of the most singularly creative and energetic persons I have ever met. She is completely dedicated to the 'proposition of possibilities' in peoples' lives, and that dedication comes shining through."
    Dan Ciporin, president,
    Dealtime.com

"The Five O'Clock Club books are 'what works now.' This indispensable, no-excuses guide to job-hunting and career building provides a step-by-step approach to organizing your search . . . targeting the job you want . . . getting in for the meetings . . . beating out the competition . . . and turning the interview into an offer."
    Jack Schlegel, New York Advertising & Communications Network

"Thank you, Kate, for all your help. I ended up with four offers and at least fifteen compliments in two months. Thanks!"
    president and CEO, large banking organization

"I have doubled my salary during the past five years by using The Five O'Clock Club techniques. Now I earn what I deserve. I think everyone needs The Five O'Clock Club."
    M. S., attorney, entertainment industry

"I'm an artistic person, and I don't think about business. Kate provided the disciplined business approach so I could practice my art. After adopting her system, I landed a role on Broadway in *Hamlet*."
    Bruce Faulk, actor,
    Manhattan (currently touring Europe in a play)

"Kate's books bring her enthusiastic, thought-provoking style to print. A must-read for every person who has a job, wants one, or may be contemplating changing it."
    Richard Schneyer, chair, Career Services Committee, Annual Convention,
    National Society of Fund Raising Executives

Building a Great

RÉSUMÉ

Kate Wendleton

with hints for new grads by Mark Gonska

http://www.FiveOClockClub.com

THOMSON

DELMAR LEARNING

Building A Great Resume, Second Edition
by Kate Wendleton

COPYRIGHT © 1997-1999 by The Five O'Clock Club, Inc.
Printed in Canada
2 3 4 5 XXX 05 04

For more information contact
Delmar Learning
Executive Woods 5 Maxwell Drive
Clifton Park,NY 12065-2919

Or you can visit our Internet site at
http://www.delmarlearning.com

For permission to use material from this text or
product, contact us by
Tel   (800) 730-2214
Fax   (800) 730-2215
www.thomsonrights.com

Library of Congress Cataloging-in-Publication
ISBN 1-56414-433-X

NOTICE TO THE READER

Publisher does not warrant or guarantee any of the products described herein or perform any independent analysis in connection with any of the product information contained herein. Publisher does not assume, and expressly disclaims, any obligation to obtain and include information other than that provided to it by the manufacturer.

The reader is expressly warned to consider and adopt all safety precautions that might be indicated by the activities herein and to avoid all potential hazards. By following the instructions contained herein, the reader willingly assumes all risks in connection with such instructions.

The Publisher makes no representation or warranties of any kind, including but not limited to, the warranties of fitness for particular purpose or merchantability, nor are any such representations implied with respect to the material set forth herein, and the publisher takes no responsibility with respect to such material. The publisher shall not be liable for any special, consequential, or exemplary damages resulting, in whole or part, from the readers' use of, or reliance upon, this material.

Preface

Dear Reader:

Do you ever feel your résumé isn't representing you in the best way possible? You're probably right. A résumé is not just a recap of what you have done and where. It's a marketing piece that should dynamically present you just the way you want a prospective employer to see you.

Studies show that the average résumé is looked at for only ten seconds! So you want a résumé that's scannable so that the reader quickly gets your message. And you not only want a résumé that people look at, you want them to find it so compelling that they look forward to meeting you.

Building a Great Résumé will take you through the entire process of developing a résumé that's just right for you. We'll make sure you're "positioned" properly for your target market. If your positioning is wrong, your résumé is wrong, and becomes a handicap rather than a help.

This book starts with an overview of The Five O'Clock Club approach to job search. Then we'll work on your accomplishment statements—the backbone of your résumé. We'll teach you the Seven Stories Exercise, which will help you express your accomplishments in a more interesting way. You'll also learn how to describe effectively any consulting, freelance, temporary or volunteer work you may have done. That's just the beginning of how we'll make your résumé more exciting to the reader.

Then we'll work on your summary—the most important and most difficult part of your résumé. Your summary increases your chances of getting exactly the kind of job you want.

Next we'll put it all together by stepping you through lots of sample résumés. The case studies will teach you the nuances of how to *think* about résumé preparation. You'll take your important accomplishments and incorporate them into the body of your résumé, making sure the body supports the statement you created for your summary.

Finally, we'll make sure your résumé is appropriate for your level: We don't want you positioned higher or lower than where you want to be.

Be sure to look in the Index under "Industries and professions." You will then be able to find the résumés in this book that refer to your field.

Be careful not to simply copy segments of the résumés in this book. ("This one sounds just like me.") It's better to use the most important things unique to *your* background that you want the hiring manager to know.

This is the only résumé book on the market with case studies. And all the case studies are of actual people. The beginning of this book also contains a brief overview of The Five O'Clock Club job-search process. But if you really want to land that next job, or if you want to think more about your long-term career, be sure to read the other books in our series. Together, these books provide the most detailed explanation of the search process :

- *Targeting the Job You Want* tells you *where* to look for a job. It is a relatively painless way to think about the career-planning process. In addition, it contains the most comprehensive job-search bibliography around.
- *Getting Interviews* tells you *how* to get job leads—part-time or full-time, freelance or consulting. In addition, it contains worksheets which you may copy for your own use.
- *Interviewing and Salary Negotiation* tells you The Five O'Clock Club way to interview, get the offer and negotiate.

All of this information is based on the highly successful methods used at The Five O'Clock Club•, where the average, regularly attending member finds a job within ten weeks. **For a packet of information on joining the Club, call 800-538-6645 ext. 600**. Also make sure you take a look at our website: **http://www.FiveOClockClub.com**. You'll find 135 articles from past issues of *The Five O'Clock News*, the basics of The Five O'Clock Club approach to job search, information on our counselors, among other things.

We are guided by the original Five O'Clock Club, where the leaders of Old Philadelphia met regularly to exchange ideas and have a good time. Today's members are the same—they exchange ideas, operate at a high level, brainstorm to help each other, and truly enjoy one another's company.

I hope the résumés in this book will give you a feel for some of the wonderful and intriguing people I have met. That's what you want your résumé to do: to entice the reader and make him or her want to meet the author.

I thank the members of The Five O'Clock Club, people who care about their careers. Their hard work is reflected in this book. Thanks to all of our counselors. They're committed to bringing the highest-quality career counseling—along with some fun—to those who care.

Finally, thanks to you for buying this book. Your appreciation of these materials makes it possible for us to continue this effort. Our goal is, and always has been, to provide the best affordable career advice. And, with your help, we will continue to stand by you to help with your career.

Cheers and good luck!

Kate Wendleton
New York City

The
Five
O'Clock
Club®

Table of Contents

Building a Great RÉSUMÉ

PART ONE

THE FIVE O'CLOCK CLUB METHOD OF JOB SEARCH

Getting Up to Speed

You've got to think about "big things"
while you're doing small things,
so that all the small things go in the right direction.
Alvin Toffler
Newsweek, April 4, 1988

The importance of a long-term
perspective cannot be overstated.
It can make the difference between a career of major
contributions and one characterized by early burnout.
Savvy managers typically seem to have
a longer view than other managers.
Joel M. DeLuca, Ph.D.
Political Savvy

When most people think of job-hunting, they think "résumé." And certainly a résumé is an important ingredient. After all, I devoted this whole book to résumés! But a résumé is only part of the process that you will see below. What's more, a good résumé is usually the result of a thorough evaluation (or assessment) where you have identified specific job targets (industries and fields), and learned to position yourself to look desirable to hiring managers in those target areas.

On the other hand, you usually need a résumé just to get started in the job-search process—even before you may clearly know the industries or fields you want to target.

It's fine to take a crack at a résumé without going through the assessment—just understand that you have skipped an important step that you should return to later, and that there are several other steps that follow the writing of a résumé.

As your targets become clearer, you may want to revise your résumé to create a better match between you and your targets.

The Job-Search Process

The charts in this chapter outline each part of the process. It's best to do every part, however quickly you may do it. Experienced job hunters pay attention to the details and do not skip a step.

The first part of the process is **assessment** (or evaluation). You evaluate yourself by doing the exercises in our book *Targeting the Job You Want*, and you evaluate your prospects by doing some preliminary research in the library or by talking to people.

Assessment consists of the following exercises:
- The Seven Stories Exercise
- Interests
- Values
- Satisfiers and Dissatisfiers
- Your Forty-Year Vision

If you are working privately with a career counselor, he or she may ask you to do a few additional exercises, such as a personality test.

First say to yourself what you would be;
and then do what you have to do.
Epictetus

Assessment results in:

- a listing of all the targets you think are worth exploring, and
- a résumé that makes you look appropriate to your first target (and may work with other targets as well).

Even if you don't do the entire assessment, the Seven Stories Exercise is especially important because it will help you develop an interesting résumé. Therefore, we have included that exercise in the next chapter.

Research will help you figure out which of your targets:

- are a good fit for you, and
- offer some hope in terms of being a good market.

You can't have too many targets—as long as you rank them. Then, for *each one*, conduct a campaign to get interviews in that target area.

Phase I: Campaign Preparation

- Conduct research to develop a list of all the companies in your first target. Find out the names of the people you should contact in the appropriate departments in each of those companies.
- Develop your cover letter (Paragraph 1 is the opening; Paragraph 2 is a summary about yourself appropriate for this target; Paragraph 3 contains your bulleted accomplishments ("You may be interested in some of the things I've done"); Paragraph 4 is the close. (many sample letters are in the other two books.)
- Develop your plan for getting **many interviews in this target**. You have four basic choices:
  - Networking
  - Direct Contact
  - Search Firms
  - Ads

You can read about each of these methods for getting interviews in our book *Job-Search Secrets*.

Phase II : Interviewing

Most people think interviews result in job offers. But there are usually a few intervening steps before a final offer is made. Interviews should result in getting and giving information.

Did you learn the issues important to each person with whom you met? What did they think were your strongest positives? Where are they in the hiring process? How many other people are they considering? How do you compare with those people? Why might they be reluctant to bring you on board, compared with the other candidates? How can you overcome the decision-makers' objections?

Interviewing is one of the most important and yet most overlooked parts of the job-search process. It is covered in extensive detail in the other two books.

Phase III: Follow-Up

Now that you have analyzed the interview, you can figure out how to follow up with each person with whom you interviewed. Aim to be following up with six to ten companies. Five job possibilities will fall away through no fault of your own.

What's more, with six to ten things going, you increase your chances of having three good offers to choose from. You would be surprised: even in a tight market, job hunters are able to develop multiple offers.

When you are in the Interview Phase of Target 1, it's time to start Phase I of Target 2. This will give you more momentum and insure that you do not let things dry up. Keep both targets going, and then start Target 3.

Develop Your Unique Résumé

Read all of the case studies in this book. You will learn a powerful new way of thinking about how to position yourself for the kinds of jobs you want. Each of the résumés in this book is for a unique person aiming at a specific target. You and your exact situation are not in here. But seeing how other people position themselves will help you think about what you want a prospective employer to know about you.

After you look at the charts, we'll start gathering important information about you—through the Seven Stories Exercise.

Phases of the Job Search
and the results of each phase

ASSESSMENT

Consists of:
- The Seven Stories Exercise
- Interests
- Values
- Satisfiers and Dissatisfiers
- Your Forty-Year Vision

Results in:
- As many targets as you can think of
- A ranking of your targets
- A résumé that makes you look appropriate to your first target
- A plan for conducting your search

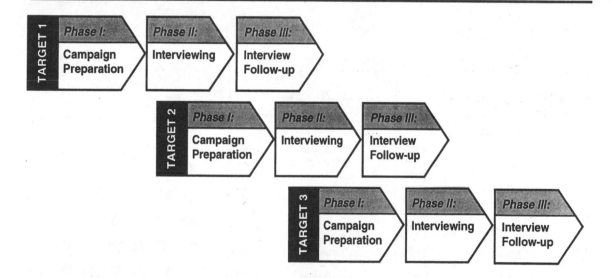

TARGET 1
- Phase I: Campaign Preparation
- Phase II: Interviewing
- Phase III: Interview Follow-up

TARGET 2
- Phase I: Campaign Preparation
- Phase II: Interviewing
- Phase III: Interview Follow-up

TARGET 3
- Phase I: Campaign Preparation
- Phase II: Interviewing
- Phase III: Interview Follow-up

RESULTS

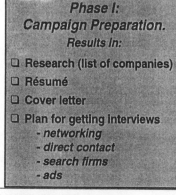

**Phase I:
Campaign Preparation.**
Results in:
- ❑ Research (list of companies)
- ❑ Résumé
- ❑ Cover letter
- ❑ Plan for getting interviews
  - networking
  - direct contact
  - search firms
  - ads

**Phase II:
Interviewing.**
Results in:
- ❑ Giving them information to keep them interested in you
- ❑ Getting information so you can "move it along"
- ❑ Plan for follow-up (You may do several in-depth follow-ups with each person)

**Phase III:
Follow-Up.**
Results in:
- ❑ Aiming to have 6 to 10 things in the works, and

Job Offers!

Four ways to get interviews in your target market

1. Search Firms
2. Ads
3. Networking
4. Direct Contact:
   - *Targeted Mailing*
   - *Direct Mail Campaign*
   - *Cold Calls*

Plan to contact or meet the *right* people in *every* company in each of your target areas—as quickly as possible.

Get meetings with people in your target areas through:
- Search Firms
- Networking
- Ads
- Direct Contact

Do not think of these as techniques for getting *jobs*, but as techniques for getting *interviews*.

- After a networking meeting, be sure to keep in touch with the person you met.
- After a job interview, think about what you can do next to turn the situation into a job offer.

COMPANIES IN THIS TARGET MARKET	BUILD RELATIONSHIPS	FOLLOW-UP
Company	Contact(s)	
Company	Contact(s)	
Company	Contact(s)	
Company	Contact(s)	
Company	Contact(s)	
Company	Contact(s)	
Company	Contact(s)	
Company	Contact(s)	
and so on ...	Contact(s)	

When you have a meeting, build a relationship: — find out about them; let them know about you.

Figure out how to move each of them along.

The Five O'Clock Club®

PART TWO

ACCOMPLISHMENTS: THE BACKBONE OF YOUR STORY

Elizabeth: What a Difference a Story Makes

*Concentrate your strength against your
competitor's relative weakness.*
Bruce Henderson,
Henderson on Corporate Strategy

Every résumé has a pitch—although it may not be what the job hunter wants it to be. In scanning Elizabeth's "before" résumé, we can easily see that she has had communications and advertising positions in a number of computer companies. That's the total extent of her pitch. When she went on interviews, managers commented: "You sure have worked for a lot of computer companies." Her résumé read like a job description: She wrote press releases, product brochures, employee newsletters, and so on.

Thousands of people can write press releases, so citing those skills will not separate Elizabeth from her competition. But we can get to know her better if she tells us about specific accomplishments.

Elizabeth agreed to do the Seven Stories Exercise. She didn't feel like writing down "the things she enjoyed doing and also did well" because she felt as though she kept doing the same things again and again in every company for which she worked, and she enjoyed them all. Still, I urged her to be specific—details can make a résumé more interesting. And working on the Seven Stories Exercise is a sure way to develop a strong overall message.

She started with an experience on a job early in her career. She had thought of a terrific idea: Her company's product could be sold through the same computer systems that were used to sell airline tickets and car and hotel reservations. She convinced the company to let her go ahead with the idea, promoted it to travel agents across the country, and also to the salespeople in her own company. It was so successful, it became the standard way to sell foreign currencies when people were going on a trip.

Most job hunters tend to ignore accomplishments that took place when they were young. But if you had accomplishments early in your career, they

may be worth relating because they let the reader know that you have always been a winner.

I said, "That sounds great. Where is it on your résumé?" Elizabeth said: "Well, it's not said exactly that way. . . " Many times job hunters are constricted when they write their résumés, but the Seven Stories Exercise can free them up to express things differently. So we restated that accomplishment.

Elizabeth then worked on another story. She had participated in a conference that had "generated 450 letters of intent."

I said: "It's nice the conference generated 450 letters of intent. But from what you said, I can't tell that you had anything to do with those results, and I don't know if 450 is good or not. Tell me more about it."

Elizabeth said: "There were only 1,500 participants in the conference, and 450 letters of intent is a lot because our product is very expensive. I had a lot to do with those results because I developed an aura of excitement about the product by putting teasers under everyone's hotel door every morning.

"And before the conference, I had sent five weekly teasers to everyone who planned to attend. For example, one week, I sent each person a bottle of champagne. This direct-mail campaign had everyone talking about us before the convention started. People were asking one another whether or not they had gotten our mailers. When they got to the convention and found teasers under their doors, they were eager to come to our booth.

"I also trained the teams of employees who were demonstrating the product at the convention. I made sure that each demonstrator delivered the same message."

Now I understood how Elizabeth had played a major part in generating those letters of intent.

Next we needed to think of the message behind this accomplishment. Was her message that she could stick mailers under doors? Or send out bottles of champagne? No, her message was that she knew how to launch a product, and that's what we put on her résumé as the main point for that accomplishment.

In her "before" résumé, Elizabeth said that she wrote press releases and did direct-mail campaigns. Her "after" résumé gives us some examples of what she accomplished with those efforts, and gives us a feel for her ingenuity and hard work.

The Summary

After we reviewed all of her accomplishments, we tackled the summary. What was the most important point Elizabeth wanted to get across? It wasn't just that she could write press releases and speeches, or do direct-mail campaigns.

She had to think hard about this. The most important thing was that Elizabeth was a key member of the management team. She sat in on meetings when the company was discussing bringing out a new product, or planning how to handle a possible crisis. Elizabeth would not be happy—or effective—in a job where she simply wrote press releases. She needed to be part of the strategy sessions.

What you put on your résumé can both include you and exclude you. A company that does not want the communications person included in those meetings would not be interested in Elizabeth—but then, she wouldn't be interested in them either.

In her summary, instead of highlighting the companies she had worked for, Elizabeth highlighted the industries represented by those companies. She listed Information Services and High-Tech first, because they represented areas of greater growth than Financial Services did.

Elizabeth was—and wanted to be again—a corporate strategist, a crisis manager, and a spokesperson for the corporation. That's how we positioned her.

In every summary in this book, the reader can tell something about the writer's personality. It is not enough that someone knows what you have done, they also need to know your style in doing it. For example, a person who had run a department and doubled productivity could have done it in a nasty, threatening way, or could have motivated people to do more, instituted training programs, and encouraged workers to come up with sugges-tions for improving productivity. Your style matters.

Look at this case study, and then do the Seven Stories Exercise. Come up with accomplishments that will interest your reader. Let him or her know what to expect from you if you are hired.

In Elizabeth's case, we hope the hiring manager will look at her résumé and say: "That's exactly what I need: a corporate strategist who knows how to handle crises, and can also serve as a spokesperson for us."

This is the response you want the reader to have: "That's exactly the person I need!" Look at your résumé. What words pop out? Is this how you want to be seen? If not, let's get going.

ELIZABETH GHAFFARI

207 Dobbs Ferry   Home: (609) 555-6666
Phoenix, AZ 44444

EXPERIENCE

ORANGE COMPUTER SYSTEMS   1994 - Present
Director Corporate Communications

Plan and supervise all corporate communications staff and activities for diversified financial information services company on a global basis.

- Develop, direct and implement global media, public relations, and internal-communications programs in support of corporate and sales objectives, working closely with executive management team.

- Direct all media-relations activities related to new product introductions and product enhancements; initiate media contacts; respond to press inquiries; coordinate and conduct interviews; and develop all press materials.

- Develop and direct advertising and promotional literature activities, overseeing all corporate publications, including corporate and product brochures, sales materials, and customer and employee newsletters.

ELECTRONIC DATA SYSTEMS   1992 - 1994
Manager, Advertising and Promotion

Developed and implemented marketing and promotion strategies for Reuters and its North American subsidiaries.

- Worked with market and product managers to identify opportunities for product and sales promotions and new product development for multiple market segments. Conducted market research, developed marketing strategies and implemented tactical plans (e.g., direct response marketing and sales incentive programs).

- Responsible for planning biannual securities analyst meetings and communication product information to investors and industry analysts.

- Orchestrated six product introductions during three-month period, including public-relations activities, promotional literature and training materials.

- Responsible for forecasting and maintaining $4.0 million budget.

- Managed corporate and product advertising programs, hiring and working with various agencies.

CREDIT LYONNAIS   1990 - 1992
Corporate Investment Officer and Product Manager

Planned and directed the sales and promotion efforts for the bank's corporate and correspondent sales staff for a variety of products including foreign exchange and precious metals.

- Developed active and profitable business relationships with correspondent banks for sale of precious metals and foreign exchange products.

- Established and developed new account relationships. Brought in eleven new corporate accounts which produced significant business in precious metals and foreign exchange trading areas.

- Managed market study to identify size, segments and opportunities of various markets. Prepared analysis and recommendations for new product development and trading vehicles.

WASSERELLA & BECKTON   1985 - 1990
Director of Marketing

Managed all activities of the Marketing Department, including product development, sales promotion, advertising and public relations activities for diversified financial services company.

- Conceptualized and developed national marketing strategy for foreign exchange services offered to travel industry professionals via automated airline reservation systems.

- Developed and implemented business plans for a variety of products, including responsibility for product positioning, pricing, contracts, advertising and promotional materials.

- Promoted from Foreign Exchange Trader to Marketing Representative to Director of Marketing in three years.

EDUCATION

B.A., Psychology, University of Phoenix   1985

ELIZABETH GHAFFARI

207 Dobbs Ferry
Phoenix, AZ 44444

Residence: (609) 555-6666
Work: (493) 345-7777

CORPORATE COMMUNICATIONS EXECUTIVE
with 14 years' experience in

- **High-Tech**
- **Information Services**
- **Financial Services**

Experience includes:

- Global Media and Investor Relations
- Customer Videos and Newsletters
- Advertising/Promotional Literature
- Employee Newsletters
- Employee Roundtables/Awards Programs
- Speech-Writing/Papers/Public Speaking

- **<u>A corporate strategist and key member of the management team</u>** with extensive knowledge of financial markets.

- **<u>A crisis manager</u>**: bringing common sense, organizational skills, and a logical decision-making process to solving sensitive, time-critical problems.

- **<u>A spokesperson for the corporation</u>**: developing and communicating key corporate messages accurately and convincingly, under deadline pressure, to multiple audiences including employees, the media, customers and investors.

**Proven team leader and troubleshooter with highly developed
analytical, organizational and strategic planning skills.**

ORANGE COMPUTER SYSTEMS

1994 - Present

<u>Director, Corporate Communications</u>

- Gained extensive positive media coverage in conjunction with launch of company's first product for new market segment.
  - Planned and conducted **<u>media events in 8 countries</u>**.
  - Resulted in **<u>positive stories in 30 major publications</u>** and trade press: *The Wall Street Journal, The New York Times, Barron's, The Financial Times, Forbes* and various foreign publications.
  - A first for the company, **<u>positive TV coverage in the United States</u>**: CNN, CNBC, **<u>and Europe</u>**: Sky Financial Television, Business Daily, The City Programme.
- Successfully **<u>avoided communications crisis</u>**, gained positive press coverage and customer support when company sold a major division. Within a 60-day period:
  - Planned and managed all aspects of a **<u>13-city, interactive teleconference</u>**.
  - Developed all written materials including various employee and customer communications, background materials and press releases.
  - Wrote speeches for six executives including both company presidents (present and acquiring companies).
  - Wrote and produced an extensive question-and-answer document covering **<u>union, compensation and benefits issues and business rational.</u>**
  - Selected and trained staff representatives for each of 13 cities.

ORANGE COMPUTER SYSTEMS, contd.
<u>Director, Corporate Communications</u>, contd.

- Developed and implemented <u>company's first employee awards program</u> for service excellence.
  - Honored employees who participated in planning sessions.
  - <u>Led to changes in key areas</u> including improvements in software manufacturing efficiencies, shortening of the product development cycle, and improved employee morale.

- <u>Introduced desktop publishing</u> program for in-house production of all promotional materials and various customer and employee newsletters.
  - <u>Reduced outside services expense by 75%.</u>
  - Created new <u>corporate standards manual</u> and reorganized promotional literature system to replace inconsistent product literature.

- Conducted group and individual <u>employee meetings</u> to gain and disseminate critical information in identifying and resolving employee-relations problems.

- Prepared quarterly management reports and written/oral presentations to top management and employees to describe corporate accomplishments compared to goals.

- Managed all customer/media/employee communications for sale of three business units.

ELECTRONIC DATA SYSTEMS   1992 - 1994
<u>Manager, Advertising and Promotion</u>

- Prepared written and oral <u>presentations to boards of directors</u> and senior managers on various services, concepts and results.

- Planned <u>product launch</u> and company participation in global foreign exchange conference. Successful product launch resulted in <u>generating 450 letters of intent from 1500 participants</u>. Assured successful product introduction:
  - Developed 5-week <u>direct-mail campaign</u> to stimulate interest and create an aura of excitement around product prior to conference. Campaign continued at conference with daily newsletter and door stuffer.
  - Maximized impact of <u>product demonstrations</u> through use of compelling visual presentation and environment.
  - <u>Trained teams</u> of product demonstrators to assure that information regarding benefits and features would be delivered in consistent way.

- Strengthened company relationships with <u>industry analysts and investors</u> by arranging product demonstrations in conjunction with bi-annual industry analyst meetings. Demonstrations stimulated interest and <u>gained support for strategic direction from investor community</u> by communicating important strategic and product information.
  - Selected products to be demonstrated, developed promotional materials, organized display area, selected and trained product demonstrators to assure delivery of consistent corporate message.

CREDIT LYONNAIS   1990 - 1992
Product Manager

- Established and developed new account relationships.
  - Brought in **11 new corporate accounts during 10-month period** producing significant business in precious metals and foreign exchange trading areas.

WASSERELLA & BECKTON   1985 - 1990
Director of Marketing

- **Developed breakthrough idea to sell** foreign exchange services (currency and travelers' checks) through travel agents the same way hotel space and airline tickets are sold — **via automated airline reservation systems**.
  - Sold concept to senior management and **negotiated contracts with three major airlines**.
  - Developed sales and operational procedures. **Hired and trained 10-person sales and operations staff.**
  - **Promoted concept to travel agents** across the country through industry trade shows and sales program.

EDUCATION

B.A., Psychology, University of Phoenix, 1985

The Seven Stories Exercise

This exercise is an opportunity to examine the most satisfying experiences of your life and to discover those skills you will want to use as you go forward. You will be looking at the times when you feel you did something particularly well that you also enjoyed doing. It doesn't matter what other people thought, whether or not you were paid, or when in your life the experiences took place. **All that matters is that you felt happy about doing whatever it was, thought you did it well, and experienced a sense of accomplishment.** You can even go back to childhood. When I did my own Seven Stories Exercise, I remembered the time when I was ten years old and led a group of kids in the neighborhood, enjoyed it, and did it well.

This exercise usually takes a few days to complete. Many people review different life phases in order to capture the full scope of these experiences. Most carry around a piece of paper to jot down ideas as they think of them.

SECTION I:

Briefly outline below *all* the work/personal/life experiences which meet the above definition. Come up with at least twenty. We ask for twenty stories so you won't be too selective. Just write down anything that occurs to you, no matter how trivial it may seem. Try to **think of concrete examples, situations and tasks, not generalized skills or abilities**. It may be helpful if you say to yourself, "There was the time when I . . ."

RIGHT	WRONG
• Got extensive media coverage for a new product launch.	• Writing press releases.
• Delivered speech to get German business.	• Delivering speeches.
• Coordinated blood drive for division.	• Coordinating.
• Came in third in the Nassau Bike Race.	• Cycling.
• Made a basket in second grade.	• Working on projects alone.

1. _____

2. _____

3. _____

4. _____

5. _____

6. _____

7. _____

8. _____

9. _____

10. _____

11. _____

12. _____

13. _____

14. _____

15. _____

16. _____

17. _____

18. _____

19. _____

20. _____

21. _____

22. _____

23. _____

24. _____

25. _____

SECTION II:

Choose the seven experiences from the above which you enjoyed the most and felt the most sense of accomplishment about. (Be sure to include non-job-related experiences also.) Then **rank them**. Then, for each accomplishment, describe what *you* did. Be specific, listing each step in detail. Notice the role you played and your relationship with others, the subject matter, the skills you used, and so on. Use a separate sheet of paper for each.

If your highest-ranking accomplishments also happen to be work-related, you may want them to appear prominently on your résumé. After all, those were the things that you enjoyed and did well. And those are probably the experiences you will want to repeat again in your new job.

Here's how you might begin:

Experience #1: Planned product launch that resulted in 450 letters of intent from 1,500 participants.

    a. Worked with president and product managers to discuss product potential and details.

    b. Developed promotional plan.

    c. Conducted five-week direct-mail campaign prior to the conference to create an aura of excitement about the product.

    d. Trained all product demonstrators to make sure they each presented our product in the same way.

    e. Had a great product booth built; rented the best suite to entertain prospects; conducted campaign at the conference by having teasers put under everyone's door every day of the conference. Most people wanted to come to our booth.

        —and so on—

People cannot let others limit their imagination of what it is they want to do or can do. Otherwise, we would never have discoveries or advance.
Mae C. Jemison, physician, chemical engineer, and America's first black woman astronaut

Action may not always bring happiness, but there is no happiness without action.
Benjamin Disraeli

In the next section, we'll get started on your résumé. First, you'll read some general guidelines and see a couple of examples of how job hunters have implemented them. Then you'll work on your accomplishments, including any relevant experience that you had while you were a consultant, freelancer, temporary worker, or volunteer.

After that, we'll "position" you to look appropriate for that next move by developing your summary statement, which goes at the top of your résumé. It's the most important thing your reader will see, and it's also the most difficult part to do well. That's okay. You will have lots of summary statements to look at, so you will be able to develop one that is right for you.

Finally, we'll put it all together by looking at the résumé case studies for people at your level. They will help you understand the thinking and the strategy that go into a really great résumé.

PART THREE

DEVELOPING
YOUR RÉSUMÉ

General Résumé Trends and Guidelines

. . . for while history does not teach that honesty, in this world, is the best policy, it surely teaches that dishonesty ultimately is the worst policy.
John Lukacs
A History of the Cold War

Your résumé is the equivalent of a sales brochure. It is not supposed to tell every detail, but to entice the reader—grab his or her attention.

Your résumé softens the reader. It predisposes him or her to think of you in a certain way, so that when you meet, he or she will already have a preconceived notion about you. Tailor your résumé to make the impression you want. Most people never consider using their résumé to create a certain impression of themselves; they simply write down their work experience. Job hunters who think of their résumé as a tool for communication tend to be more effective than those who play it safe and use a bland approach. Your credentials and experience are only one half of what you are selling. Your style and personality are the other half.

Your résumé can serve as a guide to the interview. If you highlight certain areas in your résumé, the interviewer cannot help but ask about them. If you play down or even leave out certain things, you reduce the chances of having the interview center on those areas.

This chapter will present some new thoughts on résumé writing. Some ideas may suit your style; others may not. Use what you want. But do not reject these ideas too hastily: If you have not been as successful as you would like, you may find it useful to try a different style.

What Happens to Your Résumé

Make yourself necessary to someone.
Ralph Waldo Emerson

Your résumé crosses the desk of someone. This person is not looking to hire, but something about your résumé or cover letter strikes a responsive chord. If one of your achievements addresses the reader's problems at the moment, you may be called in.

The reader says to his or her secretary, "Ask this person to come in for a chat, but be sure to say that we have no openings." You are called in for an exploratory meeting.

In most cases, there truly is no specific job opening. If the chemistry is right, and if things progress smoothly, however, a position may be developed for you. This happens more often than the average job hunter may realize—and is the ideal scenario. A position created for you has the best chance of being a successful and satisfying one.

The Purpose of Your Résumé

Your résumé serves a number of purposes:

1. It is your marketing piece.

It's important to realize that your résumé—your brochure about yourself—*will be looked at for only ten seconds.* You must make that ten seconds worthwhile. The reader will usually look at the top of the first page, and perhaps glance at the rest. You want him or her to see your opening paragraph—your summary—and other parts that you intend to stand out. If something sparks the reader's interest, he or she may spend a little more time on your résumé.

We don't care whether they do more than glance at your résumé. *What we care about is whether or not they call you in for an interview.* At this point, you are not looking for a job—you are looking for a meeting to have the opportunity to explore what is going on in their company and tell them more about you. You want to build a relationship and see if perhaps there is a place for you *in the long run.*

2. It is your sales tool in your absence.

After you leave the meeting, the manager may want to discuss you with someone else. Your résumé can speak for you in your absence and convince that second person that you have a lot to offer.

3. It can guide your interview.

The interviewer is likely to ask about those sections you've highlighted. We each have things we'd like to talk about and things we'd rather not. Emphasize:

• things you have done well and also enjoyed

If any man wishes to write in a clear style, let him be first clear in his thoughts;
and if any would write in a noble style, let him first possess a noble soul.
Goethe

doing and would like to do again;

• areas that make you more marketable by differentiating you from your likely competitors;

• areas that support your "pitch"—the main argument you are advancing about yourself;

• things you think will sell you and will be of interest to the readers in your marketplace.

The Typical Résumé: Historical

Most résumés are historical documents. They list the positions a person has had and what was done in each position. It's as if the résumé writer were saying: "I've put it all down. Now you figure out where I fit in or what I should be doing next."

But if the reader doesn't "get it"—doesn't figure out in just ten seconds what you could do for him or her—you will be passed over.

A good résumé allows readers to imagine you working in their company. Something in the résumé grabs them, and they can see some as-yet-undefined possibility for you.

Your Résumé: Strategic

Your résumé should not be a historical document, but a future-oriented, strategic one. It should select from your background and highlight those areas you want to offer and state them in ways that relate to the needs of the market.

• What kinds of things would you like to do next?

• What do you have to offer that the market may also want?

• And what do you have to offer that may give you credibility or negotiating leverage (as in "I'll do this for you, providing you allow me to do this other thing.")?

Your Résumé is Completely Under Your Control

An unlearned carpenter of my acquaintance once said in my hearing: "There is very little difference between one man and another, but what little there is, is very important." This distinction seems to me to go to the root of the matter.
William James, "The Importance of Individuals"

You have complete control. Determine exactly what will hit the reader's eye on each page, and the impression you want him or her to have of you. For example, you may want to appear to be a person with a certain background. Be sure to mention that area in your summary and highlight it in the body of your résumé. You may want to stress your long-term managerial experience, or your technical expertise. Your résumé can show that you are the kind of person who constantly comes up with new ideas and implements them, or solves problems for the company.

Tell the reader outright the kind of person you are. Most résumés focus on credentials, but with so many qualified people vying for the same position, a résumé with personality is more readable and stands out. Résumés that are detached and cold are not as effective as those that seem more human. Résumés and cover letters should be alive and enthusiastic.

What you write predisposes the reader to see you in a certain way. If, for example, you describe yourself as dynamic, the interviewer will tend to see that part of your personality. You will not have to work as hard to come across as dynamic. Even if you feel you're not acting very dynamic that day, do not be surprised if the interviewer happens to mention how dynamic you are.

This is your story. It is one you want to be proud of. Don't be boring about it.

General Guidelines for Writing Résumés

1. Before you start, do yourself a favor. Go back and do the Seven Stories Exercise. The effort you put into this will dramatically affect the quality of your résumé. It will give you the substance you need to work with, and add depth and detail to your résumé in those areas you want to highlight. It will also loosen you up and increase your chances of telling a good story about yourself.

Whether I'm working with someone making $20,000 a year or $400,000, they each go through this exercise. Then I have a better idea of what they may want to emphasize on their résumés, and what they'd rather not highlight. If your past accomplishments are important to you, they should take up some room on your résumé.

2. Most people need only one résumé. However, you can modify your résumé to make it suitable for other targets. And if your targets are completely different (such as being a customer service manager or a chef), you will probably need two completely different résumés.

If your résumé positions you the way you want to be positioned, it's a good résumé. If it doesn't, it's not good.

---

3. Aim to have a reverse chronological résumé (starting with your most recent job). Functional résumés are organized by type of work done rather than by dates. They are usually written to hide something, and they are looked upon with suspicion. Chances are, there is a way for you to say what you want to say without resorting to a totally functional résumé. For example, try a chronological résumé that has a particular job broken down functionally—that is, by the different types of work done.

4. <u>You will probably want to have a summary statement on your résumé</u>. It's an opportunity to dramatically influence the way the reader sees you and the rest of the information you have included. Take advantage of this powerful tool. But remember, it's not easy. (The cover letter is your other opportunity for positioning, to influence what the reader notices in your résumé.)

Job Target

They are able because they think they are able.
Virgil

In developing your résumé, your job target must be clearly in your mind. Major changes in your target may require different résumés. Minor changes will not.

With your target in mind, go through the accomplishment statements you developed. Select those that support your job target, and leave out those that do not support it.

If the accomplishments that best support your goal occurred a long time ago, select excerpts from them and put the excerpts in your summary. This will make it easier for the reader to see that you have had that experience.

Though you have your target clearly in mind—*do not* put it on your résumé. Your résumé could then exclude you from the hiring process.

People sometimes use a "job objective" statement to describe the kind of job they want to have next. However, if you do this, it may seem as if you only want a specific position. It can *limit* your search. Even if you are open to other positions, it may seem that you are not.

On the other hand, if you know exactly what you want, and if there are plenty of jobs with the title you are going after, then it is all right to put a job objective on your résumé.

An objective statement is also appropriate is when the job hunter wants to reassure the hiring manager that he truly is interested in the area he is looking at.

. . . my experience says that it is possible to study and imagine where we may be headed.
By imagining where we are going, we reduce this complexity, this unpredictability which. . .
encroaches upon our lives.
Peter Schwartz, *The Art of the Long View*

Your Summary Statement

In differentiation, not in uniformity, lies the path of progress.
Louis Brandeis

The summary statement sets the tone and highlights the theme—the threads that bind your accomplishments. Your summary statement describes what makes you qualified and yet different from others who may be aiming for the same position.

The summary statement goes at the top of your résumé, after your name, address, and phone number. It brings all your accomplishments together. If in your summary statement you want to say that you are a financial wizard, your accomplishment statements must support this.

Consider <u>**underlining and boldfacing**</u> what

you want the reader to see in the summary. Remember, the reader scans the highlighted parts and then reads the rest of the summary. Highlighting makes some people uncomfortable. They fear it makes them look too aggressive. But in fact you're doing the reader a favor, by helping him or her figure out where to look next.

First, Decide the Story You Want to Tell

Form follows function. Decide the story you want to tell a specific target market, and tell it as briefly as is sensible. Then decide what format to use.

The Format

I don't like work—no man does—but I like what is in work—the chance to find yourself.
Joseph Conrad

Your résumé should be attention-getting in an understated way, and readable. Lines of type that go clear across the page from one margin to the other are difficult to read. Use bulleted accomplishments to break up the text.

Think about what will show up on the first page. Your summary is most important. If the jobs you want the reader to see are also on the first page, that's lucky. But if the jobs you want the reader to see are on the second page, be aware that you will wind up with a longer summary because you should include information in the summary about those jobs that don't appear until later.

This can happen when the situation you are in right now does not lend itself to where you want to go next. In that case, format your résumé so the reader's eye will see your summary, skip over your most recent job, and go directly to one before that. Simply boldface or underline phrases in your summary and in the body of the résumé to highlight the job you want to call attention to.

The top of page two is also important. When the reader turns the page, that is the first thing he or she will see. So make sure you have something important at the top.

Scan your résumé to see where your eye natu-rally goes. That is the message your reader will get too.

The Length

Your résumé should be as long as it has to be, and no longer. Cut and cut until you cannot cut any more. You do not care if anyone ever reads your entire résumé; the fact is that he or she probably won't read it all, whether it is two pages long or five. You simply want the reader to stop at your résumé and spend more than ten seconds on it, so perhaps you will be called in.

My own résumé happens to be three to four pages long—I feel it has to be to say what I want to in the way I want to say it. I could cram it into two pages—but instead I make it attractive and readable, and *use as many pages as necessary.*

I get *lots* of interviews, even though interviewers almost invariably tell me that my résumé is too long: One thing *everyone* claims to know about job hunting is that a résumé should be no longer than two pages. That is not necessarily so. Many people mistakenly think a shorter résumé is more likely to be read, so they force a lot of information into one completely unreadable page. It is better to have a longer résumé that is scannable and readable.

The Trends in Résumé Length

In the "old days," just a few years ago, résumés were one page long. It made sense then. Most people had worked at the same company—and often the same job—for most of their careers. They were expected to stay put. Their entire history could usually fit on one page.

Those who changed jobs were often limited to doing again what they had done before. Things have changed dramatically in the past few years. Today, the average American has been in his or her job only four years, and the average person getting out of college today can expect to have twelve to fifteen jobs in a lifetime. Simply listing all the jobs one has had could easily take an entire page— without even mentioning what one has done in those jobs.

Furthermore, the job-hunting market has

Say all you have to say in the fewest possible words, or your reader will be sure to skip them;
and in the plainest possible words or he will certainly misunderstand them.
John Ruskin

---

become more sophisticated and competitive. Hiring managers are seeing more and more résumés. Yours has to stand out. It takes a certain amount of space to tell your story in a way that shows how you are different from the competition. If this makes your résumé more than one page long, that's fine.

The Trend in Dates: Put Them on the Right

Job hunters used to put the dates of employment down the left side of the résumé. But now, with people having so many jobs, there might be a string of dates down the left-hand side. Since the reader's eye naturally goes to the left column, the dates become the main message. That's why the trend these days is to put dates on the right.

Do What is Appropriate for Your Level

In the examples on the following pages, a very senior executive may have a one-, two-, three-, or four-page résumé. It depends on how complicated the person's message is.

However, a junior person should never have a three- or four-page résumé. It is inappropriate, and makes the person look silly. One page—or two at most—is appropriate.

Middle managers almost always require two pages, and sometimes three, to tell their stories in a way that is clear.

Test Your Résumé

I applied to banks. I have never seen
men on Wall Street in such complete agreement
on any issue as they were on my application.
A few actually laughed at my résumé.
Michael Lewis, *Liars Poker*

You need to test what you have written. First, show your résumé to a friend. Ask him to describe in ten seconds how the information comes across. If your friend describes you the way you wanted to come across, then your résumé is presenting you properly. If you come across as having expertise in a field that you did *not* want to highlight, then your résumé needs to position you better.

The most valuable comments are *strategic* in nature. If your friend wants you to change the third word on the second page, *it will not help you get a job.* But if he tells you that you come across as a junior accountant, when you actually headed up a division of a company, that is valuable feedback. Or if you come across as a salesperson, when you hate sales, that is valuable. It is also important for you to know if you come across as being at a higher or lower level than you really are.

Your Phone Number

List a daytime phone number. If you have an answering machine or voice mail, you can list the number as "213-555-1212 (message)"; interviewers will then expect to leave a message but not necessarily talk to you. Do the same if you use the number of a relative who is taking messages for you.

Job Titles

You must be accurate in stating your job title, and sometimes that means *not* using the title your company gave you. Use a title that truly reflects the job you held—one commonly understood outside your company. For example, if your company calls you a Programmer C, is that a high-level programmer or a low-level one? It would be better to call yourself a junior programmer or a senior programmer—titles that make more sense to the outside world.

I had a client whose job title was Marketing Representative, yet what she did was market analysis. Since she was applying for positions in market analysis, the title was holding her back—and it was also misleading. Until she agreed to change her title and make it more honest, readers thought she was in sales.

One job hunter had trouble in her search because her most recent job title was Marketing Manager, when what she had actually done was sales. She had to convince the prospective employer that in reality she had had ten years of sales experience—not marketing. Her title misrepresented her and was a handicap.

Think seriously about your company-dictated

Perseverance is a great element of success.
If you only knock long enough and loud enough at the gate, you are sure to wake up somebody.
Longfellow

job titles and make sure they truly represent what you did. If they do not represent what you did and the way you want the market to see you, you must change them to make your résumé depict you more honestly. Just be certain that your accomplishments support whatever title you use.

Reporting Relationships, Company Descriptions

Sometimes your reporting relationship gives a good indication of your level of responsibility. If it helps, put it in. For example: "Report directly to the president."

It may help to put in parentheses what your company does. For example: "Complex, Inc. (a computer software company)."

Highlighting or Understating Job Titles

Look at the first job listed on your résumé. Which would be more important to the *reader:* your job title or the name of your employer? Decide which you want the reader to notice for each position. You do not have to be consistent: In one case, it may be your title; and in another, say, if you're looking within the same industry, it may be the name of your employer. Or you may want to highlight both or play down both.

Emphasize or deemphasize by using caps, spacing, underlining, boldface, and positioning on a page. I list one job that was a bore for me at the bottom of page two of my résumé. Both my title and the name of the company are simply written in upper- and lower-case. Nothing stands out. The result is that most interviewers don't ask me about that job.

Here are some examples of highlighting:

Assistant Researcher, ACME CORPORATION
Assistant Researcher, **ACME CORPORATION**
ASSISTANT RESEARCHER, Acme Corporation
ASSISTANT RESEARCHER, Acme Corporation

This practice is effective and not offensive. It helps in the readability and the dynamism of your résumé. When it's done correctly, the interviewer will tend to talk about what *you* want to talk about.

The Date Your Most Recent Job Ended

If you have recently left a job, or know that your job is ending, should you highlight that fact by putting an end-date on your résumé, or should you say "to present"? For example:

Assistant Researcher   1993 to present
Acme Corporation

or

Assistant Researcher   1993 to 1997
Acme Corporation

Do whatever feels right. You do not want to be "rejected on paper." You need to make sure that your résumé supports you, not hurts you.

You don't have to have a résumé that is completely up-to-date. If you are now unemployed, you may want to pretend that you wrote your résumé while you were in your last job. If the interviewer asks if you are still there, you can answer truthfully that you are not—but at least you have gotten in for the interview.

Most people do not have completely up-to-the-minute résumés. Let me give you an example. At one point in my career, I was called in for an interview and was asked to bring along my résumé. Because I had been at my current company for over three years, my résumé was out of date. I was so busy, I had no time to write a new one. At the meeting, I explained what I had been doing at my present job for the past three years.

These days, being out of work has little stigma attached to it—so do whatever makes you comfortable. However, if you have been out of work for a while, you are facing a different issue: What have you been doing lately? This issue is addressed in our book *Job-Search Secrets* in the chapter "How to Handle Difficult Interview Questions."

Rank Your Accomplishments

Within each job, list first the accomplishment most important to the *reader*. If your most important one is listed last, the reader may never get to it.

Where to Spend Your Energy

On the first page—especially the summary.

Many of life's failures are people who did not realize how close they were to success when they gave up.
Thomas Edison

How to Decide If You Should Put Something on Your Résumé

Always use this philosophy: If it helps your case, put it in. If it does not help your case, leave it out.

The Question of Telling Your Age

If you are older, the accepted practice is that you would not give a clue in the résumé about your age. But the reader will invariably try to guess how old you are anyway. If, for example, you leave out your years of graduation, it will make your age look like an issue, and the reader may guess that you are older than you are. When I was applying for management positions years ago, my résumé made me sound younger than I actually was—I had worked for a few years before completing my undergraduate work. It helped my case to put my date of birth in my résumé, because I wanted employers to know how old I really was. Admittedly, this is not the usual situation. Look at your own situation to see if putting in dates would help your case or not.

Use the Language of Your Target Market

Restate your background in terms your target market will understand. If you're looking outside your company, don't lapse into company jargon; if you're looking outside your industry, don't lapse into industry jargon. For example, if you want to switch from education to a training position in the corporate world, remember that the corporate world does not have "teachers"; it has "trainers" or even "instructors." Consider using these words instead. Do not expect the reader to translate the terminology. Show that you understand his or her industry.

Is This Résumé Good or Bad?

Now take a look at the sample résumés. You'll see that it is difficult to judge whether a résumé is good or bad unless you know the circumstances and the pitch the person is trying to make.

People show me résumés all the time and ask me to tell them quickly if they are good or bad. Usually, the ones lacking summary statements are not very good. And those written with large, dense paragraphs are difficult to read, causing the messages to get lost. But other than that, I frankly cannot tell if a résumé is good or bad. I need to know more about the person and his or her goals.

If your résumé positions you the way you want to be positioned, it's a good résumé. If it doesn't, it's not good. I hope the case studies in this book will show you the power of a correctly positioned résumé—one that places you at the proper level and highlights the right areas from your background.

Some people have never seen a positioning statement at the top of the résumé and they're reluctant to use one. "Gee, are you sure that's okay? I've never seen that before. It seems too much to me."

We recommend the positioning statement because it's based on hard research. We have tracked what works for job hunters for 14 years. Thousands of Five O'Clock Club members have landed better jobs faster because their résumés *positioned them accurately and powerfully*.

Unlike other résumé books, this one is geared to showing you the reasoning behind the résumé. My clients have been delighted to learn the difference a good résumé can make in their searches. And I am delighted to pass on some of this wisdom to you.

Wally:
Not a Kid Any More

If you have a job without aggravations,
you don't have a job.
Malcolm Forbes

The price one pays for pursuing any profession or
calling is an intimate knowledge of its ugly side.
James Baldwin

Wally's approach in writing his résumé used to be okay for someone just getting out of school: He stated a career objective, which was followed by his education and then a historical listing of his work experience. Today we live in an age of sound bites and résumé overload. It would have taken the reader too long to figure out what level Wally was at, the important things he had done and where he might fit in.

Wally's "after" résumé has a summary, which makes it easy for the reader to figure out exactly what he does, and his level. In addition, the reader gets a feel for Wally's personality: "an innovator with people, processes, and equipment." Wally's old résumé told us nothing about his work style.

Wally had one more problem: the large number of jobs he had held. On the "before" résumé, the dates down the left drew attention to his job changes.

A number of those job changes were easily explained, but Wally didn't get the chance to explain them because prospective employers jumped to conclusions. Wally was "rejected on paper." He had written something a prospective employer might object to. Do not allow your résumé to defeat you. Handle those objections "on paper."

In this case, Wally inserted—in small type—the reasons he left a number of those jobs: the company moved, closed, or other explanations that do not reflect on Wally at all. The explanation is not included for every job—just enough to let the reader know that Wally would and could have stayed longer if the circumstances had been right.

With so many companies in trouble these days, a job hunter may change jobs several times through no fault of his or her own. It *may* be best to let the reader know those reasons—on paper. But don't overdo it and feel compelled to put in a reason for every job you've left.

Finally, the "after" résumé is scannable. It is now two pages long, but the reader is more likely to notice the things Wally thinks are important.

WALLACE M. PETERSEN
20 Midwood Road
Strathmore, New Jersey 05555
Telephone: 609-555-3412

Height: 5'10"
Weight: 185 lbs.
Birth date: Dec. 22, 1960
Married - 3 children

CAREER OBJECTIVE:

To gain a position with a firm that offers a challenging opportunity which utilizes a background of actual press work combined with supervisory responsibilities and an opportunity for advancement.

EDUCATION:

CAMDEN COLLEGE, Blackwood, NJ
Associate Degree in Business Administration
Major: Business Management; Elective: Two years of Spanish

EXPERIENCE:
Dec. 1995 to present

BUCKMASTER ASSOCIATES, Ivytown, PA
Responsible for creating a web-printing operation, which involved traveling the country to locate, negotiate, purchase, erect and manage the operation, which consisted of two web presses, one sheet-fed press and a prep room, which included an Opti-copy Camera-Imposer. Other duties included negotiating with vendors for best supplies and prices and building a competent work force which stressed high production <u>and</u> quality with low operating cost. Very successful and efficient.

Oct. 1988 to
Dec. 1995

PONTIAC PRESS, INC., Philadelphia
BERTRAM COMMUNICATIONS, INC., subsidiary

Hired initally to operate Pontiac's 4 unit, 2 folder Harris Press.
After demonstrating the ability to motivate press crews and substantially increase production in a union environment, appointed to direct and manage the press-room operations of a new experimental plant. It is widely known to have been an outstanding success.

Dec. 1987 to
Oct. 1988

A.D. WEINSTEIN LITHOGRAPH
Hollywood, FL

Pressman with extensive Heatset background on Harris M-1000, M-200, ATF, and Hantscho, all with double four-color (8 units) Butler and Wood Splicers, Tec and Offen Dryers, Combination and Double Former Folders, Sheeters, and one Ribbon Folder.

May 1982 to
Dec. 1987

MACMILLAN PUBLISHING COMPANY
Hired as Pressman's Helper. Promoted to lead 4-color Pressman. After 3 years, promoted to Working Supervisor.

Experience on Harris 845 with 4 units, Harris V-25 with 7 units, 4 butlers, 4 pass dryer, chill tower, combination folder, three knife trimmers, Martin Tensimatic unit, in-line glueing system. Four-color process work on publication and news-paper supplements. Experienced on coated offset, and newsprint paper.

June 1980 to
May 1982

ACME PRINTING COMPANY
Hired as Flyboy of Goss Community Five-unit press.
Promoted to Asst. Pressman.

Wallace M. Petersen

20 Midwood Road
Strathmore, New Jersey 05555
Residence: 609-555-3412

Summary of Qualifications

Web Press Supervisor/Manager
with 20 years' experience
and an emphasis on quality and productivity.

- **A hands-on supervisor**. Inspire workers to take pride in quality/quantity of their work.
    - Train workers to become independent, high-quality producers.
    - Select/retain the best people: self-starters with an eye on quality and productivity.
- An innovator with people, processes, and equipment:
    - Regularly develop **time-saving and cost-saving methods**.
- A **strong negotiator**: for both equipment and supplies. Resulted in substantial savings.
- Proficient in **rebuilding equipment**. Reduced machine downtime and costs.

Professional Experience

Web Operations Manager
1995-present

Buckmaster Associates **(specializes exclusively in printing jobs for other printers)**

Set up and managed a web-press operation. Company formerly had none.

- **Built a competent work-force:** stressed high production *and* quality with low operating cost.
    - As **printers for the trade**, our customers demanded the highest quality at a price where they could still make a profit reselling our work.
- Built from the ground up a cost-effective, highly productive web-printing operation.
    - Engineered the entire setup, determined the equipment needs and negotiated the purchase of used equipment.
    - Hired/managed daily operations of this **20-person shop** with two 36" web presses, one sheet-fed press, and a prep room.
- Researched nationally to locate, select, negotiate, and purchase equipment.
    - Oversaw the reconditioning/rebuilding/assembling of 7 printing units, 2 folders, 5 splicers, and 2 counter-stackers. Made it operational **within 2 months**.
    - **Saved the company $300,000** versus the price of already refurbished equipment.
    - To produce the highest-quality work, personally supervised the erection of two 36" web presses and one sheet-fed press to **tolerances of 1/1000ths of an inch**.
- Designed the prep room for good work flow (**Opti-copy Camera-Imposer**, plate burners, light tables, plate processors). **Saved $200,000**.
- Negotiated with vendors for prices usually given only to very large companies.
    - **Saved $500,000** per year.

Web Manager/Working Supervisor   1988-1995
Bertram Communications, Inc., subsidiary of **Pontiac Press, Inc.**
Set up and managed web operation, as working supervisor.

- **Payback on investment accomplished in only 14 months.**
- Developed a highly-motivated workforce.
    - The plant regularly attracted visitors who wanted to observe the operation.
    - The cleanliness of the workplace inspired pride in the workers.
- Produced **high-quality** work. Work formerly done on sheet-fed presses because of quality requirements was done on web at a tremendous cost savings.
- Developed **innovative** press folder **techniques** and conversions.

Reason for leaving: Entire plant moved to New York.

Pressman, A.D. Weinstein Lithograph   1987-1988

- Extensive Heat-set background on Harris M-1000, M-200, ATF, and Hantscho, all with double four-color (8 units) Butler and Wood Splicers, Tec and Offen Dryers. Combination and Double Former Folders, Sheeters, and one Ribbon Folder.

- A.D. Weinstein is almost exclusively a publication printer producing products such as *Time magazine, Cosmopolitan, Good Housekeeping, Eastern Review*, etc.

Reason for leaving: When mail rates went up, company could no longer compete.

Working Supervisor, Macmillan Publishing Company   1981-1987

Hired as Pressman's Helper. **Promoted to lead 4-color Pressman at age 23.**
After 3 years, promoted to Working Supervisor.

Experience on Harris 845 with 4 units, Harris V-25 with 7 units, 4 butlers, 4 pass dryer and chill tower, combination folder, three knife trimmers, Martin Tensimatic unit, in-line glueing system. Four-color process work on publication and newspaper supplements. Experienced on coated offset, and newsprint paper.

Assistant Pressman, Acme Printing Company   1979-1981
Hired as Flyboy of Goss Community five-unit press. Promoted to Asst. Pressman.

EDUCATION

Associate Degree in Business Administration, Camden College, 1981
Major: Business Management; Elective: Two years of Spanish

Andy: His Seven Stories Made the Difference

Andy worked on the West Coast for one of the largest power plants in the country. He had an engineering background, but he saw himself as different from the stereotype of an engineer in that he was very much a people person. In fact, he thought he would like to go into sales in his next job in the energy industry. That was Andy's target.

First, we analyzed Andy's #1 accomplishment from his Seven Stories Exercise. Though he ranked it #1, it wasn't even *on* his old résumé:

"Led the project to redesign the CRDM fan supports during the 1997 refueling outage. My boss said it could not be done. I convinced him to let me go ahead. We completed the project early and not only solved a structural problem but a union/management issue. Saved $3 million and avoided significant potential plant downtime."

Andy told me more and here's how we restated it for his new résumé:

- Conceived of **technological innovation** and **led 50-person project** that **solved heated union/management safety issue**.
  - Problem had been **unsolved for 10 years**.
  - **Saved $3 million** and avoided significant potential plant downtime.

If Andy had not done the Seven Stories, he would have skipped this accomplishment completely. We got rid of unnecessary jargon (CRDM fan supports) to make this accomplishment appealing to a broader range of power plants. We added drama to the accomplishment by stating that the problem had gone unsolved for 10 years. Often **you can add drama to your accomplishments by letting the reader know something about the difficulty of the situation you faced**.

Here's another one of Andy's Seven Stories:

"During the '97 refueling outage, a serious problem arose with seismic restraints on the steam generators. It would have kept the plant shut down, costing $1 million a day. I analyzed the situation, organized information-gathering sessions with relevant people and made field visits to verify measurements and conditions. I came up with a simple solution and saved the day!"

Here's how we wrote it up for his new résumé:

- During the '97 refueling outage, **selected to solve problem that would have prevented plant from starting up**, costing almost **$1 million/day and major regulatory fines**.
  - Under extremely high-pressure situation, developed simple solution to problem.
  - Achieved regulatory approval.
  - Led team to quickly solve problem.

This accomplishment was impossible to find on Andy's "before" résumé. It was buried as the sixth item in a list of seven bullets. You can see it in the "Second Draft" on the next page.

Here is how he had stated it:

"Solved operational difficulties which averted significant plant downtime and $1 million in losses per day."

That wasn't too bad, but we don't see the drama of the high-pressure situation, or his ability to get others to cooperate. In addition, he was *selected* to solve this problem. The Seven Stories helped Andy come up with words that were more alive and better expressed what he did.

Let's take a look at the progression of Andy's description of this particular job. In his first draft, before he was aware of the techniques used at The Five O'Clock Club, the write-up sounded like a job description:

A life requires thorough preparation. We must rid ourselves of the idea that there's a short-cut to achievement.
George Washington Carver, former slave who transformed the pattern of agriculture throughout the South

---

First Draft of Sample Accomplishment

Project Manager, Nuclear Power Department

- Responsible for the engineering and design of plant modifications and the development of plant drawings for installation.
- Conceived, created and provided implementation support for numerous plant improvements and modifications.
  Assisted Construction and Maintenance personnel in solving problems related to the installation of plant modifications.
- Interfaced with other departments (Maintenance, NS&L, Operations, QA, Tech. Svcs.) on sensitive issues concerning regulatory inquiries.
- Coordinated department schedule and prioritized engineering projects.
- Performed operability analysis on critical plant components.

Second Draft of Sample Accomplishment

In his second draft, completed after he was aware of The Five O'Clock Club techniques but before I started coaching him, Andy tried to take an accomplishment-oriented approach, which worked much better:

Project Manager, Nuclear Power

- Managed the engineering, design and installation of critical plant modifications costing from $50,000 to $6 million.
- Directed contractor and company workforces in high-pressure, schedule-sensitive $60 million refueling/maintenance outage.
- Revitalized engineering department and rearranged the way we did business for increased productivity.
- Coordinated the efforts of various departments for the accomplishment of project objectives.
- Conceived, created and organized the implementation of numerous plant advances and improvements.
- Solved operational difficulties that averted significant plant down-time and $1 million in losses per day.
- Played major role in achieving world record breaking performance at Stockton Light Station. The plant is now one of the lowest cost nuclear generating stations in the world.

I never hit a shot, not even in practice, without
having a very sharp, in-focus picture of it in my head.
Jack Nicklaus, as quoted by Jack Maguire, *Care and Feeding of the Brain*

After focusing on his Seven Stories, Andy wrote his final draft, which looked like this. Notice that we took what was his very last bullet in his second draft and highlighted it. It is a strong statement and an overview of what he did in that job. It will certainly grab the reader's attention.

Final version of sample accomplishment

<u>Project Manager</u>, Nuclear Power

Played major role in making Stockton Light
<u>**one of the best performing, lowest cost nuclear plants in the world.**</u>
<u>**Plant broke the world record for continuous operation.**</u>

- Conceived of **technological innovation** and **led 50-person project** that **solved heated union/management safety issue**.
  - Problem had been **unsolved for 10 years**.
  - **Saved $3 million** and avoided significant potential plant downtime.
- During the '97 refueling outage, **selected to solve problem that would have prevented plant from starting up**, costing almost **$1 million/day and major regulatory fines**.
  - Under extremely high-pressure situation, developed simple solution to problem.
  - Achieved regulatory approval.
  - Led team to quickly solve problem.
- Managed the engineering, design and installation of critical plant modifications ranging from **$50,000 to $6 million**.
- Revitalized the engineering department and rearranged it for increased productivity.

The write-up of that job is now looking pretty good. This restatement better emphasizes Andy's interpersonal skills as well as his knowledge of plant operations, positioning him well for a sales position in the energy field. What's more, by completing this part, Andy has already rewritten a major segment of his résumé.

Andy worked on the other accomplishments from his Seven Stories Exercise and then restated each job they were part of.

Next, he needed to write the summary statement. Below is the first draft of his summary, which he had written before he knew The Five O'Clock Club approach.

First Draft of summary

Skills	Interpersonal Communication, Negotiating, Problem Solving, Planning, Project Coordination, Supervisory, Team Leadership, Writing, Public Speaking
Education	**MBA**, Rensselaer Polytechnic Institute, Troy, New York
	MS, Nuclear Engineering, Rensselaer Polytechnic Institute, Troy, New York
	BS, Physics, SUNY at Stony Brook, Stony Brook, New York
	AAS, SUNY at Farmingdale, Farmingdale, New York

Like the story he had read to them so many times, of the poor couple who
were given three wishes and wasted them, he had not wanted enough.
James Salter, *Light Years*

Andy made a good effort to jazz up his summary. This is what he wrote before we met:

Summary of Qualifications

Power industry professional with **extensive experience** in the production
of electricity and its associated distribution.
An **accomplished manager** with **excellent interpersonal skills**.
Team player who can sell ideas and achieve buy-in from others.
Logical thinker with a knack for coming up with simple solutions to difficult problems.
Skilled at financial and operational analysis for optimal decision making.
A visionary with keen insight into the emerging competitive electricity marketplace.
MBA

Andy wanted to get into sales, so he stressed skills related to that. He also wanted the reader to know that he is knowledgeable about new developments in the power industry. But after rewriting his accomplishments based on his Seven Stories, he found that he wanted a stronger summary.	I probed further: "What would you like people in the power industry to know about you? How do you see yourself as special and different from the average person in your area?" Here's Andy's new summary:

Power Industry Manager
with experience in literally every area of power generation

- In-depth understanding of plant operations, engineering, maintenance and staffing.
  - **Ran a 1000 megawatt power plant.**
- **Negotiate with independent energy producers**. First-year savings of $63 million.
- Managed the engineering, design and installation of **plant projects of up to $6 million**.
- An innovative problem solver, **skilled at financial and operational analysis**.
- Managed staff of 30. Assembled and **led teams of up to 50** in high-pressure projects.
- **BS, Physics; MS, Nuclear Engineering; MBA**

A visionary with keen insight into the emerging competitive electricity marketplace.
An aggressive, congenial manager who develops strong union/management relations.

The first line positions Andy as a "manager" rather than as a "professional." He wants to stay in the power industry, so that is also in the first line. The second line differentiates him from other power industry managers. In addition, not too many people can say that they actually "ran a 1000 megawatt power plant." That accomplishment implies a lot. His education is also unique, so we summarized it here. The italicized section at the bottom of the summary is like the tagline in an ad: It describes the way he works, and tells something about his personality. It predisposes	the hiring manager to see Andy as a certain kind of person and it complements the headline. The final summary is more scannable than the second draft. In the second draft, we see weaker words such as "extensive experience," "accomplished manager" and "logical thinker." In the final, we see punchier and more specific phrases like "Power Industry Manager" and "ran a 1000 megawatt power plant." As Andy remarked, "That pretty much says it all. The rest of my résumé supports those points." Now let's look at the final product.

Andrew Mark Waring

21 Ocean Avenue
Manteca, CA 54999

Home: (222) 555-1234
Business: (222) 556-6734

Power Industry Manager
with experience in literally every area of power generation

- In-depth understanding of plant operations, engineering, maintenance and staffing.
  - **Ran a 1000 megawatt power plant.**
- **Negotiate with independent energy producers.** First-year savings of $63 million.
- Managed the engineering, design and installation of **plant projects of up to $6 million**.
- An innovative problem solver, **skilled at financial and operational analysis**.
- Managed staff of 30. Assembled and **led teams of up to 50** in high-pressure projects.
- **BS, Physics; MS, Nuclear Engineering; MBA**

A visionary with keen insight into the emerging competitive electricity marketplace.
An aggressive, congenial manager who develops strong union/management relations.

California Power Company, Inc.

1990 to present

Project Engineer, Planning and Inter-Utility Affairs

1997 to present

Develop strategy to position company to compete in future electric industry.

- Negotiate with independent power producers. Resulted in $63 million in savings.
- Analyze system requirements and financial advantages of plant repower/retirement.
- Assess electric generating stations future costs, risks and competitive potential.
- Assist operating departments in scheduling the economic dispatch of electricity.
- Evaluate potential purchases and sales of electric capacity.
- Negotiate and prepare contracts for the exchange, purchase and sale of electricity.

Project Manager, Nuclear Power

1995 to 1997

Played major role in making Stockton Light
one of the best performing, lowest cost nuclear plants in the world.
Plant broke the world record for continuous operation.

- Conceived of **technological innovation** and **led 50-person project** that **solved heated union/management safety issue**.
  - Problem had been **unsolved for 10 years**.
  - **Saved $3 million** and avoided significant potential plant downtime.
- During the '97 refueling outage, **selected to solve problem that would have prevented plant from starting up**, costing almost **$1 million/day and major regulatory fines**.
  - Under extremely high-pressure situation, developed simple solution to problem.
  - Achieved regulatory approval.
  - Led team to quickly solve problem.
- Managed the engineering, design and installation of critical plant modifications ranging from **$50,000 to $6 million**.
- Revitalized the engineering department and rearranged it for increased productivity.

Department Supervisor, Performance Engineering   1993 to 1995

- **Selected to reorganize Performance Engineering Department**.
  - Dept. had dissension, infighting and extremely low productivity.
  - **Doubled productivity** in less than one year.
  - Initiated cutting-edge programs that **saved millions**.
  - Department became one of the **most respected groups** in the plant.
  - Created and implemented Dept. training program. **Program became the model**.
  - Boosted group morale by **creating a team and empowering individuals**.

Fast-Track Training Program   1990 to 1993
A rigorous 3-year program of rotation supervisory assignments. Positions were critical
to the reliable operation of the electric system. Presented to a panel of executives every
three months. **Achieved top rating in this elite management group**.

Chief Engineering Inspector, Kingsburg Generating Station
- Directed contractor workforces and **installed two plant computer control systems**.
- Managed the rebuilding of 300-foot high power plant smoke stack.

Supervisor, Taft Avenue Generating Station
- Managed contractor and company workforces in the overhaul of power plant
  turbine and control systems. Unit ran better than it had in 20 years.

Operations Supervisor, Kingsburg Generating Station
- Ran a 1000 megawatt power plant.
  - Initiated substantial productivity improvements in worker practices.
  - Persuaded workers to see their efforts as part of the big picture.

Supervisor, Modesto Networks
- Directed crews in the maintenance of underground cable systems and transformers.

Supervisor, Stockton Light Nuclear Generating Station
- Responsible for the testing of critical emergency safe shutdown components.

Engineer, Mechanical Engineering
- Conceived, designed and developed power plant diagnostic Expert System.

Education
MBA, with fellowship honors, Rensselaer Polytechnic Institute, Troy, NY 1990
MS, Nuclear Engineering, Rensselaer Polytechnic Institute, Troy, NY 1990
BS, Physics, SUNY Stony Brook, Stony Brook, NY, 1988
AAS, SUNY Farmingdale, Farmingdale, NY 1982

Memberships
American Association of Individual Investors
American Society of Mechanical Engineers
American Nuclear Society

Mediocrity obtains more with application than
superiority without it.
Baltasar Gracian, *Oraculo Manual*

Downplaying His Most Recent Position

As you can see from the final version of the first page of Andy's two-page résumé, he played up the second job on the page and played down his most recent job. He felt that the Project Manager job was one of the most important he had held in his life. His current job was interesting, but not as important for making his next move.

You too can highlight what you want to in your résumé and downplay other areas.

Font Size, Spacing, Underlining

Your résumé is completely under your control. You can guide the reader's eye. If hiring managers are looking at your résumé for only ten seconds, what do they see? Make sure every line is great, because if they like what they see in those first ten seconds, they will be inclined to read more.

Some résumés in this book use underlining and boldface; others do not. With most computers, underlining alone is not sufficient: The presentation looks weak, and it actually may be better to have no underlining at all. If you are going to underline something, it should also be bolded.

Remember that italicized words are more difficult to read than non-italicized. Therefore, use italics sparingly and be sure that the font size is not too small.

Use spacing between lines to break up your résumé and make it easier for the reader to make sense of it. In general, leave more space in between each job than there is within each job. Otherwise, your résumé will look like lines and lines of type with no apparent logic.

Andy's final résumé was done in 12-point type, Palatino typeface. The point sizes are different depending on the typeface. That is, 12-point New York typeface is smaller than 12-point Palatino typeface.

When Andy makes a line space with his computer by hitting the enter key, that space is 12 points because that is the font size he is using. He can make his résumé look more logical if he leaves two full 12-point spaces between his jobs rather than just one space.

Spacing fine-tuned the look of his résumé in other places. For example, after the line "Project Engineer," Andy has a small space rather than the full 12-point space he would have had if he simply hit the enter key. The line that says "Develop strategy to position company to compete in future electric industry" is followed by another small space. This makes that portion of the résumé tighter. Logical areas are drawn together more.

Andy follows the next job title, Project Manager, with a small space. The three-line summary for that job is centered and bolded, and followed by another small space. These small spaces in Andy's résumé happen to be 4 points each.

This kind of spacing tightens up the résumé and makes the jobs hang together better. Then the reader can more easily see the logic of your résumé.

The same is true in Andy's summary. The line "with experience in literally every area of power generation" is followed by an 8-point space. And the space before the tagline, "A visionary . . . ," is also an 8-point space.

If you cannot easily make these kinds of minor adjustments, do not worry about them. They are tiny refinements that ultimately make little difference except to those of us who are perfectionists about the way a résumé looks.

Making a space other than standard size (that is, 10, 12, 14 points) is easy on the Macintosh. You simply highlight the blank line you are trying to change and, depending on the software, use command-D or command-T to enter in a different font size. Four points is usually the smallest font size you can enter.

On an IBM-compatible, the job can be much more difficult, depending on the software. Highlight the blank line you want to change, and on some programs (such as Microsoft Word), change the font size that shows in the bar at the top of the screen (for example, change "12" to "4") and hit the return key. If this task is too much trouble, simply skip it.

Now that you have an overview of how a résumé gets put together, let's get serious about yours.

How to State *Your* Accomplishments

*The fastest way to succeed is to look as if you're
playing by other people's rules,
while quietly playing by your own.*
Michael Korda

T he results of your Seven Stories Exercise
and Forty-Year Vision help you set your
long-term direction. In order to go somewhere, you must know where you are right now.
In this chapter, you will look down and see
where your feet are. You will become more
pragmatic. What have you done so far in your
life? What do you have to offer the world?

What Do You Have to Offer?

In deciding what you *want* to offer, first list all
you *have* to offer—a menu to choose from. When you
go after a certain kind of position, emphasize those
parts that support your case. If you decide, for
example, to continue your career in the same direction, you will probably focus on your most recent
position and others that support that direction.

If most of your adult satisfactions have occurred
outside your job, you may want to change something about your work life. Someday you may
decide to change careers—most of us will have to. If
you decide to change careers, activities outside
your regular job may help you make that change.

Take my case: Twelve years ago, when I was
interested in changing from computers to advertising, I offered as proof of my ability the three years I
had spent at night promoting nonprofit organizations. My portfolio of press coverage for those
organizations was my proof. Later, when I wanted
to work as a career counselor, my proof was my
many years' experience in running The Five
O'Clock Club at night, the seminars I had given on
job hunting and career development, and so on.
When I wanted to continue working in business
management, I simply offered my on-the-job
experience in making companies profitable.

If you have available the entire list of what you
have to offer, you can be more flexible about the
direction you want to go in.

Process- versus Project-Oriented Accomplishments

Present what you have to offer in terms of
accomplishments. Tell your "story" in a way that
will provoke interest in you and let the reader know
what you are really like. Accomplishment statements are short, measurable and results-oriented.
We each handle the situations in our work lives in
different ways. What problems have you faced at
work? How did you handle them? What was the
effect on the organization?

Some of us are project-oriented and others are
process-oriented. If you are project-oriented, you
will tend to take whatever is assigned to you, break
it into "projects" in your mind, and then get those
projects done. You like to solve problems, and you
get bored when there are none. Your accomplishments will state the problems you faced, how you
solved them and the impact you had on the organization.

On the other hand, if you are process-oriented,
you like to run the day-to-day shop. You can be
trusted to keep an existing situation running
smoothly, and your accomplishments will reflect
that. You like stable situations and systems that
work. You will state that you ran a department of so
many people for so many years.

A project-oriented accomplishment could look
like this:

• Designed and directed a comprehensive
and cost-effective advertising and sales promotion
program that established the company as a major
competitor in the market.

A process-oriented accomplishment could look
like this:

• Conducted ongoing reviews of market
performance of investor-owned utility securities,
using multiple equity valuation techniques. Recommended redirection of portfolio mix to more profitable and higher-quality securities.

Developing *Your* List of Accomplishments

There are two ways to develop your complete

list of accomplishments: You can start with your most recent job and work backwards, or you can start with the results of your Seven Stories Exercise. Do whichever is more comfortable for you.

Do not worry right now if you do not like your job title, or do not even like your job. Later on, we will change your title to make it reflect what you were actually doing, and we can emphasize or de-emphasize jobs and responsibilities as you see fit. Right now, get down on paper all of your accomplishments. Then we will have something to work with.

Do not wish to go back to your youth. What was challenging then would probably not satisfy you today. Look for the *elements* of those early jobs that satisfied you. These elements can help to determine your lifelong interests.

You will feel better after you have developed your list of accomplishments. You will see on paper all that you have to offer. And your accomplishments will be stated in a way that will make you proud. Discipline yourself to do this exercise now, and you will not have to do it again.

Starting with Your Most Recent Position

Write down your current or most recent position. State your title and your company name, and list your accomplishments in that position. Rather than ranking them chronologically, rank them in the order of interest to the reader.

After refining the accomplishment statements for your present or most recent position, examine the job before that one. State your title and your company name, and list your accomplishments.

Work on as many accomplishments as make sense to you. Some people cover in depth the past ten years. If you can, cover your entire career, because you never know what may occur to you, and you never know what may help you later. In doing this exercise, you may remember jobs you had completely forgotten about—and pleasant and satisfying accomplishments. Ask yourself what it was about that job that was so satisfying. Perhaps it is another clue about what you might do in the future.

After you have listed your work experiences, list accomplishments outside work. These, too, should be short, measurable, and results-oriented. These outside experiences can help you move into a new field. In fact, that's how I and many others have made career transitions. By volunteering to do advertising and public relations work at night, I developed a list of accomplishments that helped me move from computers to advertising. In those days, my outside experience included:

- Walnut Street Theatre Gallery
  Planned, organized and promoted month-long holography exhibition. Attendance increased from fewer than one hundred visitors per month to over three thousand visitors during the month of this exhibition.

- YMCA
  Handled all publicity for fund-raising campaign. Consulted with fund-raising committee on best techniques for them to use. Received plaque in recognition.

- United Way
  Received four United Way awards for editorial work in 1979; two awards the prior year. Spoke at the United Way's Editors' Conference.

Starting with Your Seven Stories

When people start with their Seven Stories Exercise, they often find that their accomplishments are stated in a more vital way. Their résumé becomes more interesting to read— it is full of "stories." If your résumé sounds dull—and perhaps like everyone else's—try this approach. It will loosen you up.

The next chapter will get you started on this new adventure.

An adventure is the deliberate, volitional movement out of the comfort zone.
James W. Newman, *Release Your Brakes*

The Five O'Clock Club®

Start with Your Seven Stories

Start where you are
with what you have,
knowing that what you have is plenty enough.
Booker T. Washington

Let your own discretion be your tutor:
Suit the action to the word,
The word to the action.
William Shakespeare

Start with your most important story from the Seven Stories Exercise—if it was work-related. Do *not* look at what you wrote on your résumé. This is your opportunity to develop very different words from those you used on your résumé—words that very likely were stilted. Instead, brag about your accomplishments and write down what you did as if you were talking to a spouse or a friend. Chances are, this unstilted description will better capture what you really did.

Then polish up that accomplishment, and a few more. If you want your reader to know about these accomplishments, work hard to state them correctly. When you have finished refining three or four major accomplishments, you'll be surprised by how much of your résumé is already done.

You will feel more hopeful about your job search after you have completed this exercise. Your accomplishments will be stated in a way that will make you proud.

Here are a few accomplishment statements. They are written in the context of a complete job so you can see how to bullet and sub-bullet. This technique lets you avoid long, bulky paragraphs that are difficult to read. Bulleting and sub-bulleting can be used on anyone's résumé.

After you have created bullets, look them over. You may find you have too many bullets in a row—for example, a string of nine would be too long. Now see which ones go together. Certain bullets can be made into sub-bullets of others. Sub-bullets will make your résumé even more logical and readable.

VICE PRESIDENT OF MARKETING SERVICES 1989-1991

- Contributed to 3 consecutive years of record 9.7% growth.
- Developed marketing and sales **training programs for 5,000 employees**.
    - Program changed "hard sell"/reactive selling to consultative and entrepreneurial approach.
    - Program shifted selling culture and positioned company for growth in the 80's.
- **Repositioned subsidiary** by redesigning logo, signage, brochures, direct- mail solicitations and collateral materials.
- Introduced customer-satisfaction measurement program that provided feedback to 1,100 branch operations and produced changes in operational procedures.

This example is written the way it would appear on a résumé. Note that certain parts are under-lined so the reader cannot miss them. It makes the résumé more scannable.

International Rescue Committee, Sakaeo, Thailand   1982-1983
Educational Programs Coordinator

Directed all educational programs in Thailand's second-largest Cambodian refugee camp, with a population of 35,000.

- Managed a budget of $300,000 and an international staff of 550.

- Conceived of and introduced programs which resulted in both a 250% expansion of participants and national recognition.

- Negotiated regularly with the Thai Government and the United Nations.

Depending on the positions he is going after, these accomplishments may be included or not. They may, for example, be unimportant for ten years, and later on become important again, depending on his job target.

Vice President, Chief Budget Officer   1996-1998
Major Not-for-Profit

Reported to Chief Financial Officer. Staff of 50 in two cities. Joined management team of new CEO and CFO to implement a more results-oriented culture in a non-profit environment.

- Coordinated annual corporate budget of $500 million expenses.
  - Introduced top-down approach, PC modeling and budget programs.
- Developed cost-allocation computer system to transfer over $200 million in indirect back-office expenses.
- Projected program costs, including . . .
  - Correcting cost allocations to collect over $2 million in additional annual revenues.
  - Saving program $3 million in potential cost overruns.
  - Developing product costs for future programs, as a member of product-development teams.
- Improved financial systems and information flow:
  - Streamlined financial reporting, **reduced cycle by 5 days**.
  - Presented strategic plan to upgrade financial systems.

Her job was basically a process-oriented job: getting things to run smoothly, reducing the reporting cycle. Process-oriented jobs can still be presented in terms of accomplishments.

Curator, Penobscott Museum   1977 - 1980

Organized all major exhibitions (5 to 6 per year) and their accompanying catalogues.

- Developed educational programs supplementing these exhibitions.
- Reorganized Museum's collection of paintings, sculptures and graphics.
- Organized special films, concerts and lectures at Museum.
- Maintained an extensive speaking schedule; promoted public relations.
- Supervised the activities of curatorial, library and installation assistants.

Avoid the crowd. Do your own thinking independently.
Be the chess player, not the chess piece.
Ralph Charell

Senior Paralegal   1992 - 1999
Burstein, Kleinder and Feld, PC

- Trained, directed and **supervised four support employees**.
- Administered, coordinated and ran secured-loan transactions.
- Served as liaison to clients and attorneys; wrote detailed progress reports.

Office Manager/Chiropractic Assistant   1992 - 1995
Dr. James Taylor

One-person office force for this busy chiropractic office.
- Transcribed own correspondence.
- Set up Leading Edge Word Processor.
- Assisted doctor with exam preparation.
- Billed patients, maintained patient files, answered phones, ordered medical and office supplies, handled appointments.

Brevard Elementary School, Parent Volunteer   1990 - 1998

- Assisted teachers with proofreading/grading students' creative writing assignments.
- Coordinated/edited newspapers for two class groups.

Her volunteer work shows that she has the experience necessary to do that next job.

Federated Department Stores   Atlanta, GA.
Sales Assistant, Summer 1990

- Sold merchandise in various departments and resolved complaints.
- Balanced daily accounts and prepared displays.

Summer jobs can count too.

Editor/Public Relations Manager, Outboard Marine   1984-1985
- Edited company magazine and handled company P.R. duties.
- Obtained publicity through most national trade magazines.
- Coordinated free-lance artists and writers around the country in producing special on-the-spot application stories about the company's products.
- Distributed innovative ideas and encouragement/promotional letters to dealers.
- Attended meetings and conventions.
- Assisted in advertising campaigns, such as photography of products.

Although he held this job a long time ago, the details are important to what this career-changer wants to do next.

It has long been an axiom of mine that the little things are infinitely the most important.
A. Conan Doyle, *A Case of Identity*

Polish up your accomplishment statements.

Rework the wording of your accomplishments. Think how they will sound to the reader. Do not "tell all." Make the reader want to meet you to find out more.

In addition, rephrase your accomplishments to make them as independent as possible of the particular environment you were working in. Make your accomplishments seem useful in other companies or even other industries.

Here is an accomplishment statement as originally written:

> **Compared the changes in various categories of revenue to the changes in various categories of labor. Plotted results on a scatter diagram to show the relationships.**

That is so boring. What were you really doing and why? Look at what you did as if you were an observer rather than the grunt working on something day in and day out. What were the results of your efforts?

Here is that same accomplishment statement reworked:

> **Defined the factors that influence profitability in professional service firms. Resulted in launch of major reorganization of company's largest division.**

Sounds better, doesn't it? The first example sounds like a person who is technical and adds up numbers all day—which is what this project was. The rewrite sounds like a person who knew what he or she was doing, had some say in how it was done and was aware of the impact on the organization—perhaps even pushed for the changes that took place in the company. The new wording makes the reader want to meet this person to learn new insights.

Here is another "before-and-after" example. The first one was not bad:

Investor Business Manager,
Middle East, Africa Division

1992 - 1993

- <u>**Reinvigorated risk-taking; improved credit practices**</u> during rebuilding of business in Gulf region. Managed relationships with selected investors.
- Helped <u>**modernize and strengthen risk management**</u> in various functions of the European division. Led a group critique of risk-management issues.

In the rewrite, the job hunter thought more about what he *really* did in the job. That became the main focus, with the details subordinate to that.

Manager, Middle East Investor Business,
Middle East, Africa Division

1992 - 1993

Redefined the opportunities in and helped rebuild Gulf Region business after years during which the company perceived high risks and low profitability. Had operating centers in 5 countries, 400+ staff.

- *Redirected marketing* to focus on clients needs as investors.
- <u>**Reinvigorated risk-taking**</u> *and* improved credit practices.
- <u>**Improved profitability**</u>.
- Designated a <u>**senior credit officer**</u> and division risk manager.

What do you want the reader to see? If you want the reader to know that you have developed training programs, does it hit the reader's eye? If you are proud of having repositioned a subsidiary and think it may be important to your next employer, can he or she find it on your résumé? You will not have to think about highlighting your résumé until it is completely put together. For now, just know that it will be an option later. This book contains many examples of accomplishment statements for people of all levels.

When writing your accomplishments:

• *Focus on results*, as opposed to the process you went through. Focus on the effect your actions had.

• *Use quantitative measures* when possible. If the quantity doesn't sound important, don't use it.

• *Show the part you played* in whatever happened to your company. If the company grew from $50 million to $200 million, were you an observer or did you have something to do with it? What was your key accomplishment?

• Don't just say what you did. *State the magnitude and the effect* it had. For example, if you say you "started up a new computer system," that statement could apply to anyone at any level. What effect did that computer system have on the company? Rework your accomplishment to say:

> Developed spreadsheet program to highlight salary inconsistencies within range. Resulted in a more equitable personnel system and savings of $100,000 a year.
> or:
> Solely responsible for the development of a computerized system that resulted in a new way to analyze accounts. Resulted in $2-million profit improvement and the renegotiation of key accounts.

Now go back and rework *your* accomplishment statements.

Other Areas to List:

Skills and equipment. If you are in a technical job, you may want to list the equipment you are familiar with, such as computers or computer languages or software, and perhaps foreign languages you know.

Books or articles written; speeches delivered. One important example implies you have done more. If you have addressed the United Nations, do not mention the speech you gave at a neighborhood meeting.

Organizations. List organizations related to the work you are seeking. If you list too many, the reader may wonder how you will have time for work.

How You Will Use Your Accomplishments List

Your list of key accomplishments will help you interview, write cover letters, and prepare your résumé. It is the raw material for the rest of your job hunt.

These are the key selling points about you— the things that will make you different from your competition. They will also whet the appetite of the reader, so he or she will want to meet you. The purpose of a résumé or cover letter is not to tell what you did, but to get interviews. During the interview, you can elaborate on what you did.

Figuring out what you really did is much more difficult than simply reciting your job description. That's the importance of doing the Seven Stories Exercise. It helps you step back from a résumé frame-of-mind so you can concentrate on the most important accomplishments of your life (in terms of what you really enjoyed doing and know you also did well). Then the exercise helps you to think about each accomplishment in

Some of us seem to accept the fatalistic position, the fatalistic attitude,
that the Creator accorded to us a certain position and condition,
and therefore there is no need trying to be otherwise.
Marcus Garvey

terms of what led up to it, what your role was, what gave you satisfaction, what your motivation was and so on.

When you write your accomplishments, think about your future and those parts of your accomplishments you may want to emphasize. And think about what you *really* did.

If You Think You Haven't Done a Thing With Your Life

Many people are intimidated when they see other people's accomplishments. They think they have none of their own. Chances are, you aren't thinking hard enough about what you have done. Even obviously accomplished people struggle to express what they have done.

If you think you haven't done much, think again. Even the lowest-level clerks have accomplishments they are proud of. At all levels in an organization, people can be presented with problems and figure out how to handle them.

Don't compare yourself with others, and don't worry about what your boss or peers thought of what you did. Maybe they did not appreciate your talents. Brag about what you have done anyway—even though your boss may have taken credit for the work you did, and even though you may have done it with others. Think of problems you have faced in your company. What did you do to handle them? What was the result for your company? Think of an accomplishment. Write it down. Then pare it down until you can show the reader what you handled and the impact it made.

Finally, don't say anything negative about yourself. Don't lie, but don't hurt yourself either. For example, never lie about where you got a degree or whether you got a degree. If you are found out, you will be fired. If you have been unemployed for a very long time, see my specific hints on how to discuss this awkward timeframe in "How to Handle Difficult Interview Questions" in our book *Interviewing and Salary Negotiation*.

For additional reading on this topic, see the chapter in this book "Résumés for People with 'Nothing to Offer.'"

Never allow your sense of self to become associated with your sense of job. If your job vanishes, your self doesn't.
Gordon Van Sauter
Former President, CBS News
Working Woman, February, 1988

The ingrained mind-set that resists change causes self-inflicted wounds, and those are the most crippling wounds of all, because they are the hardest to cure. The bottom line is: Change is irresistible; run with it.
Hedrick Smith,
Rethinking America

The ladder of success is never crowded at the top. To be a winner in any field takes hard work, discipline, and desire.
Florence Griffith Joyner,
Olympic gold medalist

Industry is a better horse to ride than genius.
Walter Lippmann

The
Five
O'Clock
Club®

How to Handle Consulting, Freelance, Temporary, or Non-Paid Work

Work is work. Experience is experience. It does not matter whether or not you were paid, or how you were paid—on payroll, as a consultant, or through an intermediary firm.

If you are performing work for a certain company but are being paid through an intermediary company, such as a temporary services firm, do not put the name of the intermediary firm on your résumé unless it is in your best interests to do so.

Companies make arrangements with intermediary firms for their own reasons, and those negotiations should not affect the way you position yourself on your résumé.

For example, Sharon is working full-time as a project manager at IBM. The project is expected to last for four years. She reports to people at IBM, works with people there and even manages IBMers. But she was hired by and is paid by a temporary services firm (and receives no benefits, by the way). Which firm should she put on her résumé: the temporary services firm or IBM? IBM is where she works. The temporary services firm is merely a middleman, and the work she does has nothing to do with them. Therefore, she should indicate that she served as a project manager for IBM. Which company actually pays her—or whether she gets paid at all—is not a résumé issue.

Here's another example: John was the manager of the mailroom at his company. The company outsourced the mail function, which means that it was now being handled by an outside firm. John stayed in exactly the same place, doing exactly the same job, working with exactly the same people as he had in the past. However, his paychecks now came from the outsourcing company instead of the place where he worked. Do not disrupt your résumé just because your company decides to handle its finances in a certain way. What if the company John worked for now decided to use a different outsourcing firm? Should he list three different companies on his résumé when he hasn't moved at all? Of course not.

In the same vein, many people gain experience by doing volunteer work. Sydney wanted to learn a new programming language. He received a severance package from his former employer and decided to quickly get some real-life experience by doing exactly this kind of work for a major corporation—for free. He said to the hiring manager: "There is no risk on your part. You get someone to work for free for a few months, and I get new experience to put on my résumé." Sydney was "hired." On his résumé, Sydney noted in his summary that he was using the new programming language and stated that he was doing consulting work for this major corporation. In fact, Sydney did the work just so he could put it on his résumé. (If you feel funny saying that you are doing consulting work when you are not getting paid, then ask the company to pay you a token amount.)

This holds true for other volunteer work you may have done throughout your life. For example, I ran The Five O'Clock Club for many years without getting paid (by my choice, all the money went to other workers). Even though I did not get paid, the experience still counted, and I happily put it on my résumé.

If you have had a number of short-term consulting assignments during a given timeframe, it is still usually better to list the companies for which you did the work rather than the company that paid you. The sample on the next page shows how one very successful job hunter did it.

By the way, you can use this same technique if you had a number of short-term on-payroll jobs. Just combine them so you don't have a long list of dates.

If you wish in this world to advance,
Your merits you're bound to enhance;
You must stir it and stump it,
And blow your own trumpet,
Or trust me, you haven't a chance.
William Schwenck Gilbert, *Ruddigore*

TIME WARNER, REUTERS, ADP   1998 - present
Project Manager

For the **REUTERS** Training and Education Department:
- **Implemented Gyrus database:**
  - Department had owned database for 2 years, but had given up on implementing it.
  - Identified steps necessary to implement, convinced management of plan's feasibility.
  - Wrote procedures manual. Trained staff.
  - **Had system up and running in two months**.

For the **TIME INC.** Corporate Finance Department
- Member of team implementing Essbase system (a state-of-the-art financial database).
  - By creating simple control procedure, **credited with saving project**.
  - Cited for providing **fast turnaround time**.
- **Provided smooth transition** in coverage for employee on leave.
  - Assumed all duties, including preparation of annual plan, monthly consolidated financial statements, cash flow statements, and analysis of ROI.

For the Controller of **ADP BENEFITS SERVICES**:
- Audited the very disorganized books of 4 acquired companies. (Books had already been audited twice, to no one's satisfaction.) **Recommended final purchase price**.
- **Revamped** the company's **billing, planning and analysis systems.**

If you do a number of consulting or freelance assignments where the names of the organizations are not significant, you may want to write it up the way it is presented below. Be sure to use numbers as much as possible to show the significance of what you did:

Employment History

Consultant   Dec. 1997 - Present
- Alliance for the Development of Salt Lake City
  - Conducting market/**feasibility study for a 6,000 sq. ft. center** for arts organizations.
- Nonprofit Technology Today, Inc.
  - Writing **newsletter for CEO's** of 1,000 United Way agencies. **Improves use of technology**.
- Other clients include: Center for Mediation and Law, Foundation for the Arts.

The Five O'Clock Club®

The Steps to Follow in Developing Your Résumé

You've already made a great deal of progress in the development of your résumé. However, let's take a break so you can see an overview of the entire process. That way, you will know where you are heading.

These steps are one way to approach the development of your résumé. They show a thought process. They are simply guidelines; you will see that even the résumés in this book do not adhere to them completely. When you know the guidelines, you will be better able to do what is appropriate for your situation. Each step is covered in much greater detail in this book.

Step 1.
Use your old résumé or develop a work history.

Use your current résumé, if you have one, as a shell for the development of your new résumé. If you don't have a résumé, write up your work history, starting with your most recent position and working backwards.

Now put this information aside until later. We don't want it to ruin your creativity.

Step 2.
Determine the target market (industry and position) in which you next want to work.

If you are at the very beginning of your search and have no target, you can use our book *Targeting the Job You Want* to figure out what kind of job you want to have next. Otherwise, you can develop a tentative résumé, which you can revise after you have identified a target market.

You will be developing a résumé for a particular target market (or perhaps closely related markets). You may need to revise your résumé for other markets. After you have completed your résumé with one market in mind, you will reexamine it to see if it works for each of your other targets. But don't worry about that now. Just focus on your first target.

Step 3.
Write out your most important accomplishments.

Write out your most important work-related accomplishments from your Seven Stories Exercise—*without* looking at your current résumé. (Be sure to see the chapter "How to State Your Accomplishments.") Polish up these accomplishments and make them the best you can. They were important to you, so chances are, you will want to have them on your résumé.

If you want the reader to value these rewritten accomplishments as much as you do, then they should take up more space on your résumé than those that are less important to you.

Step 4.
Put these rewritten accomplishments into the proper place in your old résumé.

Now take your old résumé or the work history that you developed in Step 1, and put these accomplishments in their proper place in it. Your résumé will look a little strange right now because some of it will be in your old format, and some of it will be rewritten.

Chances are, you now have rewritten a sizeable part of your résumé. At this point, *do not worry about the length of your résumé*. We'll take care of that later.

Step 5.
Rewrite the jobs of which these accomplishments are a part.

Each of your rewritten accomplishments is part of a job. Rank the accomplishments within each job. You will usually put the most important first, rather than placing them in chronological sequence.

Step 6.
Write the summary.

The very first line in your summary should make it easy for the reader to figure out what you can do for him or her. For example, the first line

Use what talents you possess: the woods would be very silent
if no birds sang there except those that sang best.
Henry Van Dyke

can be a simple that points the reader on the right track: **Accounting Manager** or **Computer Operator**.

The second line should separate you from all the other accounting managers or computer operators out there. Take a look at the next two chapters, "Writing the Summary at the Top of Your Résumé" and "Sample Summary Statements." Also be sure to see the sample résumés in the accomplishments section of this book and the sample summary statements in that section.

If you do not use a summary statement, you will be positioned by your most recent job. If you are going after exactly the same kind of position, or if the most recent position sets you up perfectly for the next one, then you *may* not need a summary.

But chances are you do. A well-crafted attractive summary catches the eye and allows you to make all of the essential points about yourself "up front," in those crucial first ten seconds. Especially if there are accomplishments early on in your career that you want to make sure the reader does not miss, you will want to use a summary.

We can't stress enough that the average résumé is looked at for only ten seconds. Regardless of the length of your résumé itself, the summary makes it easier for the reader to see the most important points, to "get it."

Step 7.
Polish up the rest of your résumé.

So far, you have:
- written out the accomplishment statements that appeared in your Seven Stories Exercise;
- reworked the jobs of which those accomplishments were a part; and
- written the summary of your résumé to make you look appropriate to your target market.

There is only a little bit left to refine on your résumé. For the remaining parts, refer again to the chapter "How to State Your Accomplishments."

Step 8.
Fix up your job titles.

Now review your job titles and company names to see how they fit in with your overall positioning. You may replace company-dictated job titles with ones that better reflect what you actually did and that may be better understood by your target market.

Step 9.
Check the message of your overall résumé.

Scan your résumé to make sure the theme you stressed in your summary runs throughout. For example, if you positioned yourself in your summary as having great sales ability, make sure the reader can easily see sales-related accomplishments in your résumé.

Step 10.
Adjust the appearance and length of your résumé.

Now you can think about the length of your résumé. To shorten it, consider the following:

- Do you have excessively wide margins? It's fine to have one-inch margins all around—or even 3/4 inch. You can also edit the line spacing. (See the case study "Andy: His Seven Stories Made the Difference" for a more detailed explanation.)

- Get rid of words that have overflowed so that they are on lines by themselves. You may have to rewrite a sentence slightly so that the statement does not overflow onto another line, but that rewrite will save you one line on your résumé. These changes can add up.

- Get rid of anything that lowers the average weight of your résumé. If you're a senior vice president, you don't need to mention that you once worked in the mail room. If you have saved a company $1 million, there's no reason to mention that you saved them $10,000 earlier. You don't have to tell the reader everything you've ever done—only the important things. However, do not mindlessly cut out the first ten years of your worklife if they may be of interest.

Cut if you're getting rid of wordiness, but *don't cut* if you're sacrificing content that helps build your case. Don't obsess about keeping your résumé to two or even three pages. One of our most successful Five O'Clock Club clients, a senior level executive, received six amazing job offers after a very short search, and she was using a *six-page résumé*. It had a great summary statement and was formatted in The Five O'Clock Club style, but even I thought it was too long.

However, when she contacted companies (through a targeted mailing, which you can read about in our book *Getting Interviews)*, they called her in. Her résumé was effective in her target market. She felt that all the experiences she recounted were important. And she did not want to cram the accomplishments to fit on fewer pages, making them unreadable.

Make your résumé as short as you can, but still make sure it is readable and scannable and doesn't omit anything important.

Your primary concern is not the length of your résumé. Your primary concern is: does it position me correctly?

Step 11.
The final scan.

Sometimes, a job hunter tells me an important accomplishment, and I look for it on the résumé. If it's there at all, often I cannot find it. When I ask the job hunter, the response usually is: "Let me look for it. I know I can find it." And only with a great deal of searching, they unearth this accomplishment. If even you have trouble finding important points on your résumé, surely the reader will also.

When someone does a ten-second scan of your résumé, what does the person see? Make sure the reader sees what you want him or her to see.

Step 12.
Test your résumé in the marketplace.

You have formed a hypothesis of how to present yourself on paper. You have decided what you think will be important to the reader and what you want him or her to know about you. Now you have to find out how others actually see you when they see your new résumé. You may find that certain statements are being misunderstood or that people see you in a way that is different from what you had planned. Adjust your résumé accordingly.

Step 13.
See the "Résumé Checklist" later on in this book.

QUOTES TO INSPIRE YOU

I made a commitment to completely cut out drinking and anything else that might hamper me from getting my mind and my body together. And the floodgates of goodness have opened upon me— spiritually and financially.
Denzel Washington, in "Spotlight: Denzel," *Essence*, November 1986

Discoveries are often made by not following instructions, by going off the main road, by trying the untried.
Frank Tyger

And Peter O'Toole told me not to play small parts, even in vehicles that would get a lot of exposure, because that would make me a small-part actor. He advised me to play leading parts anywhere—in rubbishy scripts, if need be—but play leading parts.
Michael Caine, *Acting in Film*

Writing the Summary at the Top of Your Résumé

*Greatness is not measured by what a man or woman
accomplishes, but by the opposition
he or she has overcome . . . .*
Dr. Dorothy Height, President,
National Council of Negro Women

Feel stuck in your present position? Peel off your old label, slap on a new one, and position yourself for something different.

Whether you're a branch manager who wants to go into commercial lending, or an operations person who dreams of being a trainer, the challenge you face is the same: you have to convince people that, even though you don't have experience, you can handle the new position.

It's a little like show biz: you play the same role for years and then you get typecast. It can be difficult for people to believe that you can play a different role. To move on to new challenges, you have to negotiate into the new job by offering seemingly unrelated skills as an added benefit to the employer. The key to these negotiations is "positioning" yourself.

Positioning

Simply put, positioning yourself means stating your skills and qualities in a way that makes it easy for the prospective employer to see you in the position that is open or in other positions down the road.

You may want to stay in your present company. In that case, you are positioning yourself to the person in charge of hiring for the particular department you want to enter. Or, you may want to go to a new company or even a new industry. In this case, you are positioning yourself to a new employer. Either way, the steps are the same:

1) Determine what skills and qualities your prospective employer wants.

2) Search your background to see where you have demonstrated skills and qualities that would apply.

3) Write a summary at the top of your résumé to position yourself.

4) Use the same summary to sell yourself in an interview.

Your summary says it all. It should sell your ability, experience, and personality. It brings together all your accomplishments.

The rest of your résumé should support your summary. For example, if the summary says that you're a top-notch marketer, the résumé had better support that. It's completely within your control to tell whatever story you want to tell. You can emphasize certain parts of your background and deemphasize others.

> **You can get typecast.
> To move on, you have to negotiate
> into the new job . . . by "positioning" yourself.**

Thinking through your summary is not easy, but it focuses your entire job hunt. It forces you to clarify the sales pitch you will use in interviews.

Instead of a summary that *positions,* many people use meaningless jargon—which is easy—but that doesn't position them. They claim they want "a challenging job in a progressive and growth-oriented company that uses all my strengths and abilities." That doesn't say anything at all, and it doesn't do you any good at all!

Let's consider a few examples of summaries that *will* work for you:

Pursuing the Dream Job

Jane, a client-relationship manager at a major bank, has handled high-net-worth clients for more than twenty years. She is taking early retirement and thinking about a second career. Two directions interest her: a job similar to what she has done but in a smaller bank; or, the job of her dreams—working as one of the top administrative people for a high-net-worth family (such as the Rockefellers), handling their business office and perhaps doing some of the things that involve her hobbies over the years: staffing and decorating.

If Jane were to continue on her current career path and go for a position as a relationship manager at a smaller bank, she would highlight the years she has worked at the bank. Her résumé summary would look like this:

Everything comes if a man will only wait. I've brought myself by long meditation to the conviction that a human being with a settled purpose must accomplish it, and that nothing can resist a will that will stake even existence for its fulfillment.
Benjamin Disraeli

Over 20 years handling all aspects of fiduciary relationships for PremierBank's private banking clients. Successfully increased revenue through new business efforts, client cultivation, and account assessment. Consistently achieved fee increases. Received regular bonus awards.

However, to pursue her dream job, Jane's regular résumé won't do. She has to reposition herself to show that her experience fits what her prospective employer needs. Her summary would read like this:

Administrative manager with broad experience in running operations. In-depth work with accountants, lawyers, agents and advisors. Over 20 years' experience handling all aspects of fiduciary relationships for PremierBank's private banking clients (overall net worth of $800 million). Expert in all financial arrangements (trust and estate accounts, asset management, non-profit, and tenant shareholder negotiations).

Her résumé would also focus on her work *outside* of PremierBank because these activities would interest her prospective employer: first, her work with the high-class apartment condo of which she was president for fourteen years, and then the post she held for ten years as treasurer of a non-profit organization. Finally, Jane would highlight her work at PremierBank that would be of interest to her prospective employer, such as the account on which she saved a client $300,000 in taxes.

Ready to Take Charge

Robert had worked in every area of benefits administration. Now he would like to head up the entire benefits administration area—a move to management. His summary:

14 years' experience in design and administration of all areas of employee benefit plans, including five years with Borgash Benefits Consultants. Advised some of the largest and most prestigious companies in the country. Excellent training and communications skills. MBA in Finance. An effective manager who delivers consistent results.

From Supporting to Selling

Jack wants to move into sales after being in marketing support, but he has never put a summary on his résumé. Therefore people saw him as a marketing support person rather than a salesperson —because his most recent job was in marketing support. But he had been an executive in the sales promotion area, so his new summary stresses his internal sales and marketing as well as his management experience:

10 years' progressive sales, marketing and managerial experience. Devise superior marketing strategies through qualitative analysis and product repositioning. Skillful at completing the difficult internal sale, coupled with the ability to attract business and retain clients. Built strong relationships with the top consulting firms. A team player with an enthusiastic approach to top-level challenges.

Notice how he packages his experience running a marketing department *as sales*. His pitch will be, "It's even more difficult to sell inside because, in order to keep my job, I have to get other people in my company to use my marketing services. I have to do a good job, or they won't use me again."

If you do not have a summary, by default you are positioned by the last job you held. But in Jack's case, the employer would receive the new résumé with summary and say, "Ah-ha! Just what we need—a salesperson!"

The
Five
O'Clock
Club®

Sample Summary Statements

What are the most important points you want your target market to know about you? State them in your summary. Take a look at the summaries in this chapter.

Try not to be too intimidated by what you read here. You are seeing people with their best foot forward. They may have struggled for days to come up with these summaries. Don't be discouraged. Remember that though this is the most difficult part of the résumé to write, it is also the most important. Try it, and see how well you can show off what you have done.

And be sure to look at the summaries in the résumé sections of this book. Plenty more are there, many with "before" résumés—the initial attempts people made.

---

15 years' experience as a clerk at J.C. Penney's. Stock shelves. Fill out documents. Pay attention to all details. Excellent attendance. Show up on time. Personable and pitch in to help others.

Summary of Qualifications

Over 2 years' experience in PC Development and Support. Support and advise senior management on computer needs and implementation. Experience in all areas of project management. Work well with people with varying computer abilities. Take initiative. Place high value on accuracy.

Summary of Qualifications

An honors degree in Marketing (magna cum laude) is coupled with four years of professional marketing experience and a solid history of successful projects, promotions and awards. Ability to coordinate the efforts of many to meet organizational goals. High in energy, with strong interpersonal skills.

Professional Skills

Hands-on experience within Marketing includes: Market Research, Marketing Support, Project Management, Public Speaking, Training, Computers and Vendor relations.

SUMMARY OF QUALIFICATIONS

Planning and policy professional with experience in international and government affairs. Planned and prescribed courses of action to achieve the objectives of corporate, government, and non-profit organizations. Developed policies for company's domestic and foreign businesses. Well-rounded individual with a demonstrated ability to work effectively in a variety of environments and cultures. Excellent research, communications, and interpersonal skills.

Four years of executive secretarial experience coupled with continuing college education. A solid history of excellent work relationships, both with the public and with internal personnel at all organizational levels. High in initiative and energy with strong ability to exercise independent judgment. Excellent writing skills. Trustworthy and discreet.

Professional Experience

Knowledge of PC's, both IBM and MAC
Familiar with the Internet, and with all office equipment.

But more importantly, can take on major projects and handle from initiation and planning through to implementation and follow-up.

Summary of Qualifications

A podiatrist in private practice.
A reputation for being professional, courteous and knowledgeable about state-of-the-art treatment modalities.

- Give my best to both project and patient.
- Set high standards. Thorough and detail-oriented.
- Build **excellent rapport with colleagues and patients** alike.
- Superior oral and written skills.
- From a family of doctors.
- Member, **Board of Directors**, American Red Cross, South Central L.A. Service Center

---

Experienced television journalist
with both national and international experience

- **60 MINUTES**   - **VISNEWS LIMITED**   - **CHARLIE ROSE**   - **THE FORD FOUNDATION**

Particular expertise in:

- Proposal drafting and presentation for special events and projects.
- Coverage of Capitol Hill and White House news events.
- Newsgathering, packaging and editing.
- International satellite feed coordination.

Fluent in English and Portuguese with working knowledge of Spanish.

---

8 years' experience managing facilities and support services.

Managed and developed **3 service departments** with a **staff of 40**. Reorganized and set quality standards to reduce costs and lower turnover. Implemented training programs, improved morale and the respect of workers for one another. Strong negotiation skills. Work with high technology applications. In a building of 50,000 sq. ft., responsible for **office planning, telecommunications, maintenance, and record retention.**

SUMMARY OF QUALIFICATIONS

Over 20 years' **customer-service and operations** experience with Uniroyal. Successful in managing and store operations. Also international business experience. Excellent communication and presentation skills. Speak Portuguese, Spanish and some Italian. Excellent computer skills (Uniroyal has one of the most modern computer systems). College degree. Establish a good rapport with clients of different socioeconomic levels.

---

20 years' experience in TV Production. Network and Local, Daytime and Primetime Dramatic Series. New York, Miami, Los Angeles. Intimate knowledge of scripts and work with writers. Strong production administration skills interfacing with and supervising crew, staff and budgets. Decision-maker responding to fast-paced quality production demands with a spirit of creative compatibility, stability, dedication and ease.

Program Developer and Administrator
with experience in virtually every area of counseling, education and research

Specialize in work/family issues

- Director of a counseling center **serving over 1000 clients yearly** with $500,000 budget.
- Expert in computers, quantitative and qualitative analysis.
- Supervised the implementation of hundreds of research studies.
- Published articles on aging and trauma, and children and trauma.
- Clinical Psychology, **Ph.D.**; Personnel Psychology, **M.A.**

Understand the impact of change on the employee's productivity.
Gained experience through thousands of referrals to myriad agencies for every imaginable difficulty.

A CPA/MBA with 14 years combined experience in finance, accounting and systems.
Seven years experience in the agricultural services industry.
An independent, goal-oriented problem solver with a record of success in
managing, organizing, streamlining and automating
administrative, operating and financial functions.

Twenty-five years with local, regional and national not-for-profit organizations
developing and administering self-supporting programs for members and the public.

Primary areas of interest:

- Designing programs and service-delivery systems
- Identifying and cultivating funding sources
- Recruiting and training volunteer leaders

---

11 years' experience in Juvenile Justice/Child Welfare Advocacy

- Managed staff of 60; 150 volunteers; 3 departments; budget of $2.2 million.
- Designed programs, facilities and information systems.
- Managed quality of service programs.

Set the tone for the quality of service provided by staff and volunteers.
Achieve organizational goals while maintaining excellent relationships.

Seven years' experience in all areas of kitchen management
in a variety of established restaurants.

- Chez Marguerite • Saxony Hotel • Hyatt Hotel • The Square Plate

- Resourceful and organized manager; accepted additional responsibilities that easily fit
  into an already coordinated schedule.

  - Managed staff of 7
  - trained and developed staff
  - responsible for hiring
  - conscious of food costs
  - as a motivator and teacher, inspired staff to be reliable and organized

- Worked closely with owners and management to develop menu items that fit in with
  overall scheme. **Resulted in higher sales**.

- Can provide a **variety of cuisines and methods for preparation**:
  - various ethnic orientations: French, Italian, American and so on
  - various levels of complexity; from simpler pasta dishes to foie gras and truffles

- Developed and implemented systems in all areas of kitchen:
  - operate **on schedule** regardless of interruptions or problems
  - quickly take over any area to keep production going
  - create a satisfying kitchen atmosphere
  - institute systems to maintain good sanitation habits

Degree, Culinary Institute of America
Eight years' business experience

Eight years as a <u>clinical nutrition specialist</u> in pediatrics and public health.
A solid background in basic <u>laboratory research</u>. Resourceful, persuasive, diplomatic, constructive and goal-oriented. Provide <u>consulting services to 15</u> non-profit, community and academic institutions. <u>Widely published</u> to lay and scientific audiences. Experience ranges from the care of individuals (infancy to middle-aged) to the planning of <u>national programs</u>. Have worked with all the major nutritional disorders. A specialist in the rehabilitation of failure-to-thrive children.

<u>6 years' international business/legal experience.</u> <u>Dual French and American citizenship</u>. Law degree. Have worked in Paris, New York, London. Also understand Italian, German, some Chinese. Strong interpersonal skills.

<u>Summary of Qualifications</u>

<u>General management executive</u>: <u>broadcasting, fund raising and promotion.</u>

- For over 20 years, <u>**owner/operator of two Mid-West radio stations**</u>.
  - Hosted two-hour <u>radio talk show</u> six days a week for 10 years.
- A <u>**seasoned idea-generator, fund raiser and promoter**</u>.
  - Motivate the general public to respond.
- A <u>community leader</u>.
  - <u>**Strong public image**</u> and inspire a high level of confidence.
  - Well-known and held in high regard.
  - Heavily involved in charitable and community needs.
- Resourceful, creative and ready to help.
  - <u>**Action-oriented, dynamic and persuasive**</u>.
  - Constant and loyal supporter.
- Degrees from Purdue and the University of Illinois (M.S.).

---

18 years' proven project management experience
PC computer systems, training and education, PC-based business solutions
A PC problem-solver, developer and troubleshooter

- Designed, developed and managed state-of-the-art CBT programs that significantly enhance training experience and performance of participants.
- Managed the development of unique highly marketable real-time computerized simulation.
- 18 years of teaching, training and adult education.
- During two-year period, managed company's first PC Center devoted entirely to learning a fundamental new technology.
  - Hired and managed instructor staff by matching needs of business unit to skills of instructors.
  - Trained over 500 professionals of all levels in first year of operation.
  - Taught classes in Lotus, WordPerfect, Dbase and DOS.
- Managed company's first-ever video conference for Chairman and President.

13 years' experience developing **corporate trademark promotions, special events and licensing campaigns**. Substantially increase revenues through the development of creative and unique concepts as well as detailed attention to follow-through. Extensive national, international and multi-national exposure. Interaction with CEO's of major corporations.

---

20 years' international business experience in:
- **international trade**   • **sales and marketing**   • **management**

Specialize in the Asia/Pacific region, especially Taiwan, Hong Kong and PC.

Strong business negotiation skills with Asians. Established Asian subsidiaries for three major U.S. corporations. Strong company representative for trade and operations both in Asia and the U.S. Speak nine Chinese dialects, English and Japanese. Bi-cultural. Outgoing and dedicated. Establish easy rapport with all levels of professional people. U.S. citizen.

---

18 years in Corporate/Public Affairs specializing in international programs

Work with top levels in corporate, government, international and philanthropic organizations. Routinely assigned sensitive and "impossible" major projects.

Creative Executive
specializing in the new media and entertainment industries
with more than 20 years' experience in:

- **Product Development**   • **Project Management**   • **Content Development**

- **Content Provider**: For **Internet** company providing commercial video search engine service, developed characters and concepts for corporate branding.

- **Web-Site Developer**: For **on-line community/retail web-site**, creating content, a marketing strategy and interactive game.

- **Brand Director**: As **Editor-in-Chief of Pluto Group**, Plutonium Entertainment, oversaw the **#1 best-selling comic-book character** in the country, producing annual revenues of **$46 million**.

- **Product Innovator**: As **Creative Director**, Porter and Sklark, initiated and developed new product category, producing **wholesale grosses of $90 million** over 5-year period.

Team leader and troubleshooter with proven ability to bring together ideas and talent
to create imaginative, commercially successful, high-quality products.

INTERNATIONAL HUMAN RESOURCES EXECUTIVE
Policy Development   Organizational Planning   Management Training

Over 15 years' experience in international human-resources environments. Solid capabilities in strategic planning, policy formulation, management development, succession planning, and recruitment.

Major accomplishments in improving productivity through executive development, management training, business development, and strategic planning. Additional skills in providing technical and professional assistance to start-ups in international markets.

Marketing Manager
specializing in major fund-raising/development/marketing activities/special events for not-for-profit agencies and small companies

Areas of Expertise

- Telemarketing • Broadcast Fund-raising • Direct Mail
  - Media-Stimulated Calling • Major Special Events
  - Membership/Customer/Constituency Development

- Created integrated campaigns including direct marketing, television, fund-raising, and so on.
- Managed telemarketing programs for organizations such as:
  - GTE • The United Way • UNICEF • Workforce America
- Conducted major television fund-raising campaigns.
- Managed all communications for the 1992 Democratic National Convention
  - Coordinated the work of 300 to 1000 people.

Seventeen years' experience in real estate: residential apartment acquisition and quality management, negotiating, banking relations, and contractor and tenant relations. Twenty years' experience in manufacturing including purchasing, inventory control, interpersonal relations, sales operations and quality management.

CONSUMER SALES AND MARKETING MANAGER

Areas of Expertise

- Sales Management   • Trade Shows/Sales Meetings
- Merchandising   • Sales Incentive Programs
- Telemarketing   • Pricing, Packaging, Promotions
- Brand Management   • Excellent Speaker

Managed staff of 12; $1.1 million budget. Took a brand with no exposure in the Michigan market: Grew it to $4 million within 3 months. Coordinated 2 key sales meetings and 2 retail trade shows.

Aggressive in the marketplace. Consistently a top performer.
Effectively organize and manage staff.

Hands-on Systems Manager
with strong technical competence in systems analysis and design, both batch and on-line.

- Routinely selected to manage the most critical, time-sensitive and highly visible projects.
- Experienced in both batch and on-line in a wide variety of systems, such as:
  - Financial Systems
  - Order Processing/Quality Control
  - Network Systems
  - On-line Order Entry
- Insist on quality, resulting in a smooth implementation.
- Develop creative and innovative solutions that dramatically cut development time.
- Maintain strong relationships with all levels of users.
- Strong programming background: Assembler, COBOL, 4th Generation; Honeywell, IBM.
  - Learn on the job with little formal training.

INTERNATIONAL TELECOMMUNICATIONS EXECUTIVE

Eighteen years in <u>telecommunications</u>, twelve as <u>network manager/planner</u> for <u>large end-users</u>, six years in <u>market research</u> and forecasting. Experienced researcher in <u>radar techniques</u> including <u>antennas</u> and <u>signal processing</u>.

- Presented 3-year telecom plan to company executives.
- Upgraded company-wide voice/data network.
- Implemented Unicol's voice/data network.
- MBA, UCLA; MSEE, University of Michigan; BSEE, Georgia Institute of Technology

---

An innovative strategic marketer, manager, and research scientist with 10 years at IBM.

Launched new products in a highly competitive market. In-depth understanding of business, customers, competitors and the resulting products. Ph.D. in Chemistry; undergraduate in Pre-Med. Technical consultant to U.S. Navy. Six years in Research, Development and Manufacturing.

SUMMARY OF QUALIFICATIONS

**Fifteen years' management experience with the State of California in
Data Processing, Telecommunications Networking, Computer Technology,
Data Center facilities-planning and construction.**

- Managed a network of over 300 lines, over 3000 terminals, communicating with all major State buildings.
- Coordinated reconstruction of 10,000-square-foot data center that met corporate standards.
- Planned security and implemented encryption for critical data communications lines.

**Conduct timely implementation of new lines, new technology, equipment installation and follow-up.
Excellent rapport with other managers, end users, clients, and staff.**

In the following résumé, the job hunter does not like his present job.
Therefore, in the summary he highlighted jobs he had six and ten years earlier:

Summary of Qualifications

Manager of Financial Planning and Analysis
with a public accounting background.

Industry Experience Includes:

• Retail   • Financial Services   • Transportation • Communication   • Chemicals

For Macy's:
- wrote business plans for <u>store openings,</u>
- supervised and performed financial projections and <u>analysis of sites, competitors and demographics,</u>
- <u>coordinated five-year</u> and annual plans and quarterly and monthly budget,
- **wrote business plan** of a home-center chain.

In public accounting:
- selected to develop new audit techniques, which reduced costs of major audits,
- taught national and regional audit seminars.

MBA, Finance; BS, Finance and Accounting

SUMMARY OF QUALIFICATIONS

Accounting/operations executive with over 18 years of steadily increasing diverse management experience. Complex and sophisticated environments. Strong technical and analytical skills.

- Business experience ranges from securities and credit cards to travelers checks and mortgage servicing.
- Quantitative and analytical orientation - CPA.
- Managed both line operations and staff units from 5 professionals to over 50 people.
- Extensive user involvement in development of PC-based and mainframe-resident applications.
- Developed innovative strategies and methodologies to solve major problems.

PROFILE

Regional Sales Manager
Technology-based Industries

- **Staff of 20**.   • Revenue of $30 Million
- **Consistently exceeds plan.**
  - In three years at Wal-Mart, **doubled worldwide sales** of certain core products.
  - Obtained enthusiastic support from 16 internal organizations.
- In Houston during oil bust, managed major account sales group.
  - **Took it from last place to #2 in Xerox**.
  - Brought leadership, direction and focus to a disintegrating situation.
  - Achieved **11 President's Clubs**.
- Formally recognized for assembling **the most talented sales teams.**
- Strongly believe in results-centered management.

*Develop imaginative, profitable solutions consistently
delivered with the support of challenged, committed colleagues.*

SUMMARY OF QUALIFICATIONS

A corporate trade finance and marketing executive with 10 years' international and domestic experience.

- Proven **generator of fee revenue** via financial advisory mandates.
- Structure and market cross-border trade finance solutions which **open foreign capital markets**.
- Experience in both the trading and financing of commodity trade flows.
- Identify, originate, structure and close **innovative and resourceful financial structures** for countries burdened with debt:

  - commodity/asset-based trade
  - debt swaps/liquidation
  - hedging techniques
  - commodity swaps
  - barter/countertrade/offset
  - unblocking of currencies

- Foreign sales management, product introduction and marketing experience

---

*CFO and General Manager.
Directed companies ranging from $100 million to over $1 billion.
Divisional as well as Corporate Management experience.*

Industry Specialties

- **Pharmaceuticals/Health Services**
- **Consumer Goods**
- **Publishing**
- **Manufacturing**
- **International**

Chief Financial Officer
Specializing in turning around/growing medium-sized companies.

- A key member of the management team developing growth strategies while keeping the company under control.
- Set up the corporate structure for new subsidiaries.
- Rebuilt the financial organizations of two medium-sized companies, enabling them to raise significant capital.
- Attract and retain top quality people.

Areas of expertise:

- Finance
- Administration
- Real Estate
- Banking Relationships

Industry experience includes:

- Service Businesses
- Sports
- Construction
- Chemical/Manufacturing
- Perfume
- Retail

Business Manager
with strong <u>customer-service management</u> expertise.
Over 20 years in financial services and not-for-profit

- **Created** and directed **new business** opportunities and **turned around** performance.
  - As Business Manager, **increased profits 294%** over two years. Improved service 41%.
  - As Customer Service Consultant, measurably improved service in **60 locations**.
  - As Branch Manager, increased revenue 37% in one year; significantly improved service.
- As Board member for **three not-for-profit** organizations, directed programs that provided services to children, families, and people with AIDS.

Focus simultaneously on increasing revenue and improving service.
Noted for forming exceptionally strong relationships, motivating staff,
providing leadership, direction and spirit to get the job done.
Energetic, articulate, resourceful.

Chief Legal Executive
specializing in communications, information and entertainment.

A General Counsel:
manage internal lawyers; supervise outside counsel.

A deal-maker and senior legal advisor:
key member of the management team;
sophisticated in legal, financial and business dealings.

Human Resources Generalist

- Financial Services   • Health Care   • Manufacturing

Developed new programs/services. Achieved significant cost savings. Improved and enhanced existing services. Excellent presentation, negotiating and consulting skills. High standards of integrity, professionalism and teamplay. M.B.A.

Areas of Expertise

- Organizational Development
- Employee Relations
- Succession Planning
- Performance-based Management Systems
- Employment Management

- Training and Development
- Agency Relationships
- Compensation
- Staffing and Mobility
- Affirmative Action

Financial Services Technology Head

regularly selected to manage large, challenging development efforts.
Domestic and International

- Manage staffs of 150; budget of $25 - 30 million.

- Successful experience with large, "from scratch" development efforts:, both domestically and internationally. Responsible for:
  - management of all projects dealing with front-end systems **world-wide.**
  - development and maintenance of **all systems throughout Middle East and Africa**.
  - complete re-development of all product processing and administrative systems.

- **Saved $60 million** by renegotiating major purchasing agreements

A "hands-on" senior manager with very firm technical grounding.
Lead and motivate technical staffs while developing excellent user relationships.

SENIOR CORPORATE LEGAL MANAGER

for global organization with 100+ attorneys and annual profits of $1 billion.

GTE   DUPONT   NBC

Industry experience includes:

- consumer products   • information business
- media   • communications/R&D   • chemicals, pharmaceuticals

- Senior legal advisor, **reporting directly to President and COO**.
- **Instituted and led** what culminated in a **judicial victory for entire industry.**
- **Successfully prosecuted copyright-infringement suit against major competitor**.
  - Achieved strategic goal of maintaining customers and revenues.

Recognized for reflective and open analytical methods,
astute business-counseling skills and ability to provide strategic focus
with respect to company's domestic and international consumer businesses.

Project Manager specializing in service businesses

- Managed projects of up to 120 people; budgets of up to $30 million; both domestically and internationally.

- Expert in the use of project-management software tools and techniques.

- Built diverse applications on multiple software and hardware platforms.

  - Built and implemented $20-million **integrated customer information system.** Hired and trained highly skilled project team.

  - Developed and installed a **generic package** that satisfied the needs of companies in 28 countries.

  - Managed relaunching of proprietary credit card. Total responsibility for all specifications, hardware, code development and implementation.

  - Experience as both a line and matrix manager.

  - CASE-tool experienced.

Start projects from scratch, build strong project plans and strong loyal teams.
Known for being able to resolve "impossible" problems
and motivate demoralized staff.

Audit Executive - Multinational Environment

Involved in auditing all aspects of the Corporation including Technology.
Managed Multicurrency Audit Budgets up to $20 million.
14 years' experience in interfacing with Audit Committees, Secretary since 1981.

- Managed multinational, multilingual global audit staffs—up to 340 people.
  - Able to deal with any audit issue.
  - Resources, expertise and technical skills were shared globally.
  - Put in streamlined audit processes and automated audit systems.
- Have reported directly to Chief Auditor or CEO continuously since 1978.
- Developed Audit Strategic Plan focusing on Business and Audit Risk.
  - Encouraged auditors to take prudent risks.
- Substantially improved reward systems and visibility for the Audit staff.
- Regularly address audiences of up to 200 people on Auditing Topics.
- MBA, CPA and Chartered Auditor.

Senior Sales
and Client Management Executive
with a track record of creating substantial new business income.

*Manage the start-up, turn-around, and enhancement
of corporate finance relationships and lines of business.*

• AMBRACK • HAGEN-ROGERS • WILDE-LORD

- A generalist, with a current specialization in **Telecommunications, Publishing and Information companies**.

- Significant domestic and international market experience:
  - in corporate, not-for-profit, and government agency client markets
  - in both wholesale and retail.

- Management experience in both short- and long-range planning, corporate development, risk management, project management, and building new lines-of-business.

GENERAL COUNSEL
with a staff of 40 lawyers
specializing in health law, environmental law and public policy

- Key member of management team of 2000-person organization with $500 million budget.

- Intimate knowledge of **important State and Federal government agencies** responsible for Health, Insurance, Social Services, and Environmental Conservation.

- **Negotiated a dozen landmark health laws of national significance,** major consent agreements and intra- and inter-agency agreements.

- Organized, led and reported on **major investigations of government corruption** and mismanagement. Resulted in major legislation, dismissals and program improvements.

- Serve as public spokesperson for State Department of Health on key health issues including medical malpractice, government reorganization and regulatory reform.

*Excellent judgment, high integrity.
Able to organize and motivate large groups.*

How to Write an Electronic Résumé

Y ou can have an electronic résumé simply by removing all highlighting so that it can be scanned into a computer. After your résumé is scanned in, it can be searched by companies and search firms through the use of keywords. In this computer age, some predict that scanned résumés will be the driving force in the selection process of the future. As of this writing, however, electronic résumés have had little impact on the job searches of Five O'Clock Clubbers. Let's put electronic résumés in perspective.

In our book *Getting Interviews*, you will read that there are four basic ways to get interviews in your target market: through search firms, ads, networking and direct contact. Five O'Clock Clubbers learn to consider all four techniques for getting interviews, and then to assess which approach produces the most *meetings* for them.

You should consider using search firms and ads in your job-search mix. In your particular field, they may be an important source of meetings. However, these approaches are passive: you have little control over the process. The search firm or the company that placed the ad must call you in. The use of electronic résumés is also a passive approach to job search. You must wait for someone to call you in.

On the other hand, networking and contacting companies directly are proactive approaches: *you* decide whom to contact and *you* contact *them*. While we encourage job hunters to consider every technique for getting interviews in their target markets, we want them to measure which techniques result in meetings with hiring managers. Those are the techniques you should use more. If electronic résumés result in meetings for you, then use them.

Companies Using Résumé-Scanning Equipment

Some companies have equipment that scans in thousands of résumés. Theoretically, when someone in that company wants to hire a new employee, the manager would ask for those résumés that fit the experience he or she is looking for. In real life, Five O'Clock Clubbers *are* getting jobs with compa-

nies that happen to use scanning equipment, *but they are not getting many interviews through this technology.* Instead, Five O'Clock Clubbers are getting in to see the hiring managers through networking, direct contact, search firms—or even answering ads. When you contact a company through their résumé-scanning technology, it is usually a dead end. If a company asks for a scannable résumé, give them one, but be proactive: find some other way in. That's what Five O'Clock Clubbers do. The interview is most likely to come from the "other way," not from the scanned-in résumé.

Posting Your Résumé on the Internet or Other Electronic Medium

Job hunters also use electronic résumés for answering ads on the Internet and for putting their résumés on line. To address this issue, I will quote from The Five O'Clock Club's Internet expert, Patricia Raufer. Patricia wrote the following in *The Five O'Clock News* ("The Internet as a Job-Search Tool," March/April, 1996):

Some job hunters have even created their multimedia résumé, with extensive background information; it may include video clips or samples of work—all packaged to be transmitted electronically. This method may be appropriate for creative and technical positions because it demonstrates use and understanding of the technology. Job seekers who respond online to job postings often send an electronic version of their print résumé. However, ... the electronic résumé has not replaced the standard résumé and cover letter. Using the electronic medium for communication offers the benefit of enabling you to respond quickly, but it is not necessarily the easiest method for the recipient. As with all the communications techniques in job search, choosing the right one is part of the process.

Many of the Internet career websites provide an area in which job hunters post their résumés for access by potential employers. However, access is not always limited to just employers. Therefore by posting your résumé, you're providing personal information, employment history and credentials to people whom you don't know. Would you tack up your résumé on a public bulletin board or hand it out to strangers simply because they asked for it? And how can you follow up effectively if you don't know who has looked at your credentials?

So, use your judgment about relying too heavily on electronic résumés. We all would like something magical to save us from the grueling work of searching for a job, but many of the ideas you may come across are not effective. Having said that, let's take a look at how you actually do an electronic résumé.

Making Your Résumé Scannable

If you have been using The Five O'Clock Club approach to developing your résumé, you are almost there. First of all, you have gotten rid of company jargon so the outside world can understand what you have done. You have also changed your job titles to reflect what you actually did, rather than using company-dictated titles that may not be as accurate. And you have made your résumé accomplishment-oriented—a good approach no matter what kind of résumé you have.

Electronic résumés are scanned into a database. They do not need to look pretty. In fact, you cannot have any underlining, bolding, bullets or other characters that may confuse the scanner—just use plain, straight text.

Secondly, your résumé must contain keywords that the hiring manager is most likely to search for regarding the kind of work you want to do. Therefore, at the top of your résumé, where you may have put Operations Manager, for example, add a string of words that would also be appropriate for you, like this:

Operations Manager, Administrative Manager, Accounting Manager, General Manager, Strategic Planner, Inventory Control Manager, Materials Manager, Customer Service Manager, Management Consultant.

If you have prepared your résumé The Five O'Clock Club way, the body of your résumé should be fine. Again, choose words they are likely to look for. If you are adept at computers, list the hardware and software you know. Only list software that is generally available—not the company-specific systems you may have used. For example, you may list IBM, MAC, Lotus 123 or WordPerfect. But don't list ACS, your company's Accounting Control System. That's a name that would not be recognized in the outside world.

The rest of your résumé would be the same as what you have already prepared, but without any highlighting.

Electronic résumés are just one technique which may or may not be important in your search. At The Five O'Clock Club, we suggest you consider all techniques and do what is appropriate for you.

There are fundamental differences
between training and education.
If you are trained you become the employee,
if you are educated,
you become the employer.
If you are trained you have a J.O.B.
(if you're "lucky"),
if you are educated you have a career.
If you are trained you have been taught to memorize,
if you are educated
you have been taught how to think.
Jawanza Kunjufu, *Countering The*
Conspiracy to Destroy Black Boys

It isn't possible to win high-level success without
meeting opposition, hardship, and setback.
But it is possible to use setback
to propel you forward.
Dr. David Schwartz,
The Magic of Thinking Big

The Five O'Clock Club®

PART FOUR

RÉSUMÉS FOR MAKING A CAREER CHANGE

Elliott: Getting Back Into a Field He Loved

Elliott had been in sports marketing years ago, and had enjoyed it tremendously. However, he had spent the past four years in the mortgage industry and was having a hard time getting back into his old field.

The sports people saw him as a career changer—and they saw him as an mortgage man. Even when he explained that marketing mortgages is the same as marketing sports, people did not believe him. He was being positioned by his most recent experience, which was handicapping him.

When a job hunter wants to change industries—or go back to an old industry—he cannot let his most recent position act as a handicap. For example, if a person has always been in pharmaceuticals marketing and now wants to do marketing in another industry, the résumé should be rewritten to emphasize generic marketing skills and most references to pharmaceuticals should be removed.

In Elliott's case, the summary in the new résumé helps a great deal to bring his old work experience right to the top of the résumé. In addition, Elliott has removed the word "mortgage" from the description of his most recent job; his title at the mortgage company now stands out more than the company name; and he has gotten rid of company and industry jargon, such as the job title of segment director, because it is not something easily understood outside of his company.

Notice that the description of what Elliott did for the mortgage business is now written generically—it can apply to the marketing of *any* product. With his new résumé, Elliott had no trouble speaking to people in the sports industry. They no longer saw his most recent experience as a handicap and he soon had a terrific job as head of marketing for a prestigious sporting-goods company.

If you want to move into a new industry or profession, state what you did generically so people will not see you as tied to the old.

Bring Something to the Party
When it comes down to negotiating yourself

into a new position, seemingly unrelated skills from former positions may actually help you get the job.

For example, some of my background had been in accounting and computers when I decided to go into counseling. My CFO (chief financial officer) experience helped me ease into that career. I applied to a ninety-person career counseling company and agreed to be their CFO for a while—provided I was also assigned clients to counsel. They wanted a cost-accounting system, so my ability to do that for them was what I "brought to the party." I was willing to give the company something they wanted (my business experience) in exchange for doing something I really wanted to do (counseling executives).

Combining the new with the old, rather than jumping feet first into something completely new, is often the best way to move your career in a different direction. You gain the experience you need in the new field without having to come in at the entry level. Equally important, it is less stressful because you are using some of your old strengths while you build new ones.

Coming from a background different from the field you are targeting can also give you a bargaining chip. If you are looking at an area where you have no experience, you will almost certainly be competing with people who do have experience. You can separate yourself from the competition by saying, "I'm different. I have the skills to do this job, and I can also do other things that these people can't do." It works!

In the previous chapter, you saw dozens and dozens of summary statements. In the sample résumés in this book, you can see how the summaries are used to set the tone for the rest of the résumé.

**Elliott's summary statement
is on the next page.**

For a thorough discussion of how to change careers, see our *Targeting* book to figure out what you want to do, and our *Getting Interviews* book to tell you how to do it.

Think like a duchess, act like a duchess, talk like a duchess,
and one day you will be a duchess!
Henry Higgins to Eliza Doolittle in
George Bernard Shaw's *Pygmalion*

Elliott Jones

421 Morton Street

Chase Fortune, KY 23097

Sears Mortgage Company

1995 - present

Vice President, Segment Director, Shelter Business
- Director of $4.6-billion residential-mortgage business for the largest mortgage lender in the nation.
- Organized and established regional marketing division for largest mortgage lender in nation, a business which included first and second mortgages, and mortgage life insurance.

SportsLife Magazine

1993 - 1995

Publisher and Editor
- Published and edited the largest consumer health and fitness magazine and increased circulation 175%.

and so on. . .

Elliott Jones

421 Morton Street

Chase Fortune, KY 23097

Marketing Executive
with 15-plus years in the leisure/sporting goods industry.

Domestic and international experience; multi-brand expertise specializing in marketing, new business development, strategic planning, and market research.

Proven record of identifying customer segments, developing differentiable product platforms, communication strategies, sales management, share growth and profit generation.

Sears Mortgage Company

1995 - present

VICE PRESIDENT, BUSINESS DIRECTOR
Residential Real Estate Business

- Business Director of a $4.6-billion business. Managed strategic planning, marketing, product development and compliance.

- Consolidated four regional business entities into one; doubled product offerings. Grew market share 150 basis points and solidified #1 market position.

- Developed and executed nationally recognized consumer and trade advertising, public relations and direct-response programs.

- Structured a product development process which integrated product introductions into the operations and sales segments of the business.

- Organized and established regional marketing division for largest mortgage lender in nation, a business which included first and second mortgages and mortgage life insurance.

SPORTSLIFE MAGAZINE

1993 - 1995

Publisher and Editor

- Published and edited the largest consumer health and fitness magazine and increased circulation 175%.
. . .and so on. . .

76

Carol: Moving Towards Her Dream

Carol had been in traditional bank marketing for many years. Now she wanted to think about the next move in her career. She completed all of the assessment exercises in our book *Targeting the Job You Want*.

In her Forty-Year Vision, Carol could imagine herself fifteen years from now in her own small company representing independent filmmakers and serving as the agent for actors. She imagined ten people working for her. She also imagined that her business would be international.

This exercise result was a complete surprise to her. However, years ago—before she took a sensible job in banking—Carol had worked in the arts and had even hosted a television show in Japan. In fact, it turned out that all of her friends were in the arts—not in banking. I asked Carol to give this scenario some deep thought before dramatically changing her career.

At work the next week, she was astonished to find that her co-workers were talking about someone they knew who was making an independent film and needed help. She could not believe her ears; she asked if they thought she might volunteer to help promote the film. To add to the felicity of the situation, the lead actor was an African-American—as Carol was. Part of her long-term plan was to change the image of African-Americans in films so they are not just cast as being people of color, but are cast in parts that would ordinarily go to whites.

So she volunteered to publicize this independent film, and she accomplished a lot. In fact, the film won an award at the Cannes film festival, which was partly attributed to her efforts.

Carol decided to move her career in the new direction. Perhaps she could get a day job in the entertainment industry that would mesh with what she was now doing at night.

We redid her résumé to highlight her extensive marketing experience in both banking and in the entertainment industry. She is now conducting a search aimed at the entertainment industry, and will move her career in a completely different direction.

Carol Franklin

234 Mercy Douglas Drive
Drysdale, TX 44555

Home : 555-555-1234
Work: 666-555-2312

International Marketing Executive
in the finance and entertainment industries

- Manage a P&L and the marketing function for $30 million business.
- Publicist for *Yours Truly*, an independent film. Won award at Cannes.
- Set up regional processing centers in Europe and Asia.
  - Dramatically improved customer service.
- Appeared as a regular host on Japanese television and radio.
- Speak Spanish, Japanese and French.
- Master's in Business Administration in the Arts.

Possess a combination of business sense and artistic awareness.
Known for meeting the goals at hand.

Howard: Repositioned for a New Industry

You have brains in your head.
You have feet in your shoes.
You can steer yourself
any direction you choose.
You're on your own. And you know what you know.
And YOU are the guy who'll decide where to go.
Dr. Seuss, *Oh, the Places You'll Go!*

Howard had spent his entire working life in banking. Now he needed to look for a job, but banking was retrenching. (In fact, 78 percent of the people who lost their jobs in his bank ended up leaving the banking industry.) Therefore he decided to target a growth industry—health care. But he hedged his bets by targeting banking as well.

Howard got rid of the banking jargon in his operations background, and highlighted those areas that would interest managers in hospitals and other health-care claims processing centers.

In addition, Howard seriously targeted health care by meeting lots of people in the field, joining health-care administration associations, subscribing to health-care trade journals and networking into lots of hospitals.

The changes in his résumé may seem subtle, but they made all the difference in the world. For example, the term "financial services" is dropped in the headline of the health-care summary. The first bullet on the banking summary lists operational areas specific to banking, while the health-care summary emphasizes generalized transaction processing, with no specifics.

To make it simpler, we have included here only the summaries. The body of each résumé stayed the same.

By the way, Howard ended up in an exciting job in health care.

Summary of Qualifications

*Financial Services Operations and Control Executive
with a uniquely strong data processing and systems background;
experienced in turnarounds and conversions.*

- Managed **every aspect of operations**: check processing, security processing, lockbox, charge card processing, ATM and POS settlement.

- Controlled every major financial services application: deposit accounting, trust accounting, cash management and electronic funds transfer.

- **Turned around** failing operations. <u>Built</u> management <u>teams</u>.

- Managed **large-scale systems conversions and consolidations**.

- Designed management information and **quality improvement systems**.

- **Assessed entire operations** designing new workflow and control processes.

Areas of Expertise

- Transaction processing management
- Workflow analysis
- Starting up operations

- Accounting and control
- Team building
- Planning/Restructuring

- A participative manager who builds consensus.
- As a senior manager, work effectively with top management and boards.
- Experienced and successful in turning around and starting up operations.
- A strong planner, having successfully managed large system conversions/operation consolidations.

Summary of Qualifications

Operations and Control Executive
with a uniquely strong data processing and systems background;
experienced in turnarounds and conversions.

- Managed numerous **transaction processing** operations, all high volume and computer based.

- **Developed claim tracking systems** and management informations systems that cut costs, reduced risk and improved customer service.

- Led major technical conversions, managing both systems analysts and operations personnel, in multi-million dollar computer projects.

- Implemented accounting and control methods that corrected major financial control problems.

- Assessed entire operations, designing new work flows and control processes.

- **Turned around failing operations** by building management teams and eliminating fundamental problems within the operation.

Areas of Expertise

- Transaction processing management
- Workflow analysis
- Starting up operations

- Accounting and control
- Team building
- Planning/Restructuring

- A participative manager who builds consensus.
- As a senior manager, work effectively with top management and boards.
- Experienced and successful in turning around and starting up operations.
- A strong planner, having successfully managed large system conversions/operation consolidations.

Stephen: Moving from Non-Profit to For-Profit

Even if Stephen were not trying to change careers, his is a good case study of how to restate one's accomplishments better and reposition oneself for the future. Like many people, Stephen wrote a résumé that was simply a listing of what he had done in each job, without regard to what he would like to do next.

Following the steps we recommend, Stephen did his Seven Stories Exercise and Forty-Year Vision. He thought he might like to look for work in the for-profit sector, after having spent his working life in not-for-profit. Therefore, we would need to use the jargon of the for-profit world.

When Stephen wrote out his Seven Stories, his top accomplishment was his most recent job. Here is how he related that accomplishment to me:

"I turned around a fragmented, demoralized network of thirteen volunteer-run chapters, estranged from the national organization, into a vigorous and activist network of thirty-seven chapters. The network that I formed became the driving force for 100-percent growth in national membership over eight years."

As Stephen spoke, I took notes. He was verbally positioning himself very differently from the way he had positioned himself on his old résumé. The résumé was dull, whereas the story he was telling me now was alive and dramatic. We needed to capture that drama on paper so people would understand what he really did: He turned around an organization. To dramatize the accomplishment, we showed the situation he was presented with and the result he achieved. The accomplishment statement is centered, bolded and italicized so it pops out:

Took an organization that consisted of 13 dispirited and disorganized chapters and made it into a vibrant, profitable 37-chapter organization.

On his new résumé, this sentence is the central statement in the rewrite of that job. Take a look at the rest of that job, and see how it is presented in the before and after versions.

Since his most recent job was the biggest accomplishment he had, we wanted to highlight it more than anything else on his résumé. We also made sure that the top of page 2 started with an important accomplishment. When the reader turns the page, that is the first thing he or she sees.

In working on his summary, Stephen decided that he most enjoyed starting up, growing and turning around organizations, so we made that the key sub-point in his summary statement. To make him marketable in the for-profit market, we can't use the term Associate Director. Instead, we called him a General Manager, which was a job title he had held previously in a very small organization. He thought that that title would work for both the for-profit and the not-for-profit sectors.

The first bullet in the summary tells the reader more about the general manager role he played in his most recent position: he was part of a three-person team that controlled the budget for this organization. Note that, as much as possible, we use numbers in his summary so the reader can quickly see what he has done.

Because Stephen comes across in person as very relaxed, we needed to let the reader know that, in his own way, he gets a lot done. So the italicized portion at the bottom of the summary tells us how he operates despite his laid-back demeanor.

Stephen was doing consulting work to earn money while he continued to look for the right job. Because he had been doing this for a while, he needed to put it on his résumé or it would look as though he had been doing nothing since he left his last full-time job. Again, numbers help to stress the importance of the work he did. For example, simply saying that he wrote a newsletter would not be as impressive as saying that he wrote a newsletter for the CEO's of 1000 United Way agencies to help them improve the use of technology in their organizations. Although all of this work was for non-profits, we stated it so as to appeal to for-profits.

STEPHEN CROWN
33 West South Street
Central City, Utah 99025
444-555-9814 (h)
444-555-1990, ext 234 (w)
E-mail: stcrown@aol.com

EMPLOYMENT 1991- Present	**American Institute of Design Engineers** Associate Director, Membership and Chapters

The AIDE was founded in 1918 and is the major engineering design membership organization in the U.S., with 9,000 members and an operating budget of $2,300,000.

Developed and managed a nationwide network of 37 incorporated, volunteer-run chapters, with an annual budget of $160,000. Organized the creation of 24 new chapters since 1991, including incorporation, board formation, by-laws, tax-exemption, fund-raising and committee and program development. Developed orientation and other support materials, including a management handbook, for chapter board members and volunteers. Acted as ombudsman between chapters and the national organization. Provided on-site consultation to chapters on management, planning and program development.

Responsible for long-term membership growth, from 4,500 to 9,000 since 1991, and a membership budget which grew from $600,000 in 1991 to 51,400,000 in 1999. Managed production of recruitment materials; direct mail campaigns; database installation and maintenance; and delivery of membership benefits. Wrote and produced quarterly membership newsletter.

Introduced and organized annual three-day retreats for 150 chapter leaders and national board members. Originally created to provide technical assistance to chapter leaders, the retreats evolved into the major forum for broadbased discussions of national issues and examination of the future direction of the organization.

Involved in all aspects of national conferences, including site selection, marketing, and production of events for up to 1,500.

Member of three-person management team, with staff of fifteen, responsible for all aspects of organizational development and direction, including long-range planning, strategy, and policy. Personally supervised staff of three.

1986 - 1991   **Affiliate Artists, Inc.**
Associate Director, Residency Operations

Ran national multi-discipline performing artists residency program, involving major corporate sponsors, local arts institutions, and emerging artists. Also managed $100,000 statewide program serving local arts councils, funded by the State Council on the Arts. Created and developed showcase programs in the state and elsewhere. Responsibilities included artist selection and training for residency work; selection and preparation of local presenting organizations; grant writing; and reports to granting agencies.

1983 - 1985   **Orchestra and Chorus of St. Louis, St. Louis, MO General Manager**

Founding manager of small professional orchestra and chorus with $100,000 budget and eight-concert season, specializing in rarely performed music, presented at the St. Louis Art Museum.

1982-1983   **Repertory Theatre of St. Louis and Opera Theatre of St. Louis, St. Louis, MO**
House Manager

1977 - 1981   **International House, Paris and Rome**
Teacher of English as a Second Language

EDUCATION
1975   **St. Andrew's University, Scotland**
BA, French and German

STEPHEN CROWN

33 West South Street
Center City, Utah 99025

444-555-9763
E-mail: stcrown@aol.com

General Manager

**specializing in high growth, start-up and turnaround situations
in cause-related or cultural service organizations**

- Part of three-person management team controlling a budget of $2.3 million.
  - Doubled membership from 4,500 to 9,000.
  - Grew membership income from $600,000 to $1.4 million.
  - **Created 24 incorporated chapters**.
  - Served as in-house consultant to all 37 locations.
- **Founder and general manager** of a professional orchestra and chorus in St. Louis.
- Cultivated **strong contacts with corporations** such as Mobil Oil, GE, Alcoa, Westinghouse

*Conceive the vision. Develop the plan. Implement all details.
Coordinate diverse constituencies.
Motivate and lead all levels to operate towards the organization's goals.*

Employment History

Consultant   Dec. 1999 - Present
- Alliance for the Development of Salt Lake City
  - Conducting market/**feasibility study for a 6,000 sq. ft. center** for arts organizations.
- Nonprofit Technology Today, Inc.
  - Writing **newsletter for CEO's** of 1,000 United Way agencies. **Improves use of technology**.
- Other clients include: Center for Mediation and Law, Foundation for the Arts.

American Institute of Design Engineers   1991 - Dec. 1999
Associate Director

*Took an organization that consisted of 13 dispirited and disorganized chapters
and made it into a vibrant, profitable 37-chapter organization.*

- Part of three-person management team, with a staff of fifteen, responsible for all aspects of organizational development and direction, including **long-range planning, strategy, and policy**. Personally supervised a staff of three.
- **Increased membership from 4,500 to 9,000**
  - ... and increased membership income from $600,000 to $1,400,000.
  - Implemented infrastructure for a nationwide network of 37 incorporated chapters.
  - Created 24 new chapters, including incorporation, board formation, by-laws, tax-exemption, fundraising, and committee and program development.
- Conceived of **national conference approach where all could attend**, regardless of distance.
  - Became a "town meeting" and highlight of the year for attendees.
  - Arranged conferences for up to 1,800 people.

Associate Director, contd.

- Supported/directed chapter management.
  - **Introduced systematic training** including board training and the training of volunteers.
  - Wrote and produced orientation and other support materials for chapter board members and volunteers. This included a **130-page management handbook**.
  - Conceived and organized annual three-day orientation and planning meetings for 150 chapter leaders and national board members.
  - Provided **on-site consultation** to chapters on management, planning and program development.
- Acted as ombudsman between chapters and the national organization.
- Managed production of recruitment materials and direct mail campaigns.
- Supervised data base installation and maintenance, membership processing and delivery of membership benefits.
- Wrote and produced quarterly membership newsletter.

Affiliate Artists, Inc.   1986 - 1991
Associate Director, Residency Operations

- **Ran national multi-discipline performing artists residency program**, involving major corporate sponsors, local arts institutions, and performing artists.
- **Managed statewide program** serving local arts councils, funded by the State Council on the Arts.
- Created and developed showcase programs in the state and elsewhere.
- Responsible for artist selection and training for residency work, selection and preparation of local presenting organizations, grant writing, and reports to granting agencies.

Orchestra and Chorus of St. Louis, St. Louis, MO   1983 - 1985
General Manager

- **Founding manager of professional orchestra and chorus** with eight-concert season.
  - Specialized in rarely performed music. Presented at the St. Louis Art Museum.

Repertory Theatre of St. Louis   1982 - 1983
Opera Theatre of St. Louis, St. Louis, MO
  House Manager, responsible for all front-of-house activities.

EDUCATION

BA, French and German, St Andrew's University, Scotland, 1975

MEMBER

American Society of Association Executives
Technical Assistance Providers Network

J.E. Bean: Cashing in on Volunteer Work

Promises that you make to yourself
are often like the Japanese plum tree
—they bear no fruit.
Frances Marion

Life can only be understood backwards;
but it must be lived forwards.
Kierkegaard

WILLY: *You wait, kid, before it's all over we're*
gonna get a little place out in the country,
and I'll raise some vegetables, a couple of
chickens . . .
LINDA: *You'll do it yet, dear.*
Arthur Miller, *Death of a Salesman*

J.E. was lucky: when she lost her job as a bank accounting clerk, she received generous severanucation grant. She used her time and money wisely. She went to school to study medical billing and then volunteered full time in a hospital as a medical biller. Although she was not paid, work is work, and she knew it was the experience that counted.

With six months of volunteer experience under her belt, J.E. launched a search for a full-time paid position. The important things she wanted to say about herself were described in her current volunteer position, so she didn't need an elaborate summary. The rule of thumb is this: if you do not have a summary, you are positioned by your most recent position.

In her summary, she simply listed the most important things she wanted her readers to know: her medical billing as well as her accounting background. She also included a few statements that describe her personality—the way she approaches her job. Then the reader knows not only that she accomplishes a lot, but *how* she does it.

Because J.E. is already in the field that interests her—and because she wants more of the same—she has a relatively simple story and can tell it in a relatively small amount of space.

J.E. Bean
1346 Commonwealth Avenue
Dobbs Ferry, New York 99999
(999) 555-6544

Medical Biller
with strong background in accounting and proof control

A hard working team player with a perfect attendance record

Holly Oak Medical Center   1999 - Present
Medical Billing

- Currently a volunteer in the OB/GYN
- Accurately enter patients' demographics into the Medical Manager System,
  as well as post payments and make changes when necessary.
- Verify patients' insurance eligibility.
- Abstract information from patient files for reimbursement.
- Code CPT procedures as well as diagnosis ICD'9 CM.
- Abstract demo information from ADT system for billing purposes.

Citibank
Senior Accounting Clerk   1988 - 1998
- Handled basic accounting functions. A/P, A/R, billing.
- Performed 2-way proof of debits and credits.
- Performed "back-value" calculations on mutual funds and private banking.
- Conducted heavy research.
- In securities area, worked with Paine Webber, Salomon, and other broker-dealers.
- Handled securities deliveries, fed wires and government securities, etc.
- Reconciled daily department transactions.
- Computer skills include: Windows, Word, Excel, Lotus Notes.
- An exceptional team player with great communication skills. Supported fellow co-workers.

Bankers Trust
Foreign Exchange Department, Claims Processing   1987 - 1988

Ralston-Purina   1980 - 1985
Inventory Clerk
Handled billing and collections of all incoming and outgoing merchandise and quarterly inventory.

EDUCATION

Springhurst College, 1999
Currently taking advanced medical billing

American Institute for Career Learning, 1998
Certificate in Medical Billing

International Career Institute
Merit courses in Recordkeeping, Office Practice and Procedures, and Computer Literacy

---

Paul: He *Thought* He Was Making a Career Change

Think of it like Camus's Sisyphus—he keeps pushing the rock up that hill, pushing and pushing and pushing. It never ends. But the thing you must realize is, Sisyphus is happy.
Roman Polanski, filmmaker, quoted by Robert Goldberg in *The Wall Street Journal*, 1/6/95

You get moving very quickly and you end up in the wrong place.
Marshall McLuhan
quotes by Pico Iyer,
The New Business Class

Paul had worked in the not-for-profit world his entire life, and he was now 62! He was the head of the direct-marketing arm of a major not-for-profit (the real name of his former employer is not used in the sample résumé). He felt that he was undervalued, and suspected that he was about to be squeezed out. He wanted to go into the for-profit world.

To learn more about this target area, his counselor and group at the Club suggested he read trade journals, join direct marketing trade associations and get to know people in the field. Paul learned so much in his intensive research that he went a few steps further: he *spoke* at the association meetings, began writing for trade journals and even appeared on the cover of a prestigious trade magazine.

When he first developed his résumé, Paul thought of himself as a not-for-profit specialist. But his best recourse now—whether he wanted to stay in non-profit or move into for-profit—was to emphasize what he had done in bottom-line business terms. After all, nonprofits today are run like businesses.

Paul de-emphasized the name of his former employer and even replaced his official title (which did not work well outside of his present organization). He played up the actual work he had done and made it much more bottom-line oriented.

The biggest mindset change for Paul was to stop presenting himself as a career changer trying to make a "break" into a different realm. The more he stressed "transition," the more prospective employers saw it as a problem. Paul tried a new approach: had learned so much he was able to come across as an insider. When prospective employers mentioned that all of his experience had been in the not-for-profit world, he feigned surprise. He emphasized that his presentations were primarily to those in the for-profit sector and emphasized how those in both the for-profit and non-profit worlds were following his lead.

The weakest approach is to *say* that you are trying to break into a field. The strongest approach is to show that you have already *been* in that field and simply want to get another job in that same field.

Paul A. Dorfman

777 Riverside Drive
Oswego, CA 99999

Business: (555) 555-2594
Home: (555) 555-4736

Industry-Recognized Direct Marketing Executive
with extensive database systems experience

Currently managing programs raising over **$25 million annually**

- **Reversed a declining catalog mail order business**, increasing revenue 12% in the first year and 30% in three years.
- Improved profitability of a $15 million direct mail program after a five-year decline.
- In one of the most dramatic direct mail successes in many years, developed computer software and database support for an increase in presidential-year revenue from $2.5 to $12.5 million.
- Recently interviewed by "Newsweek on Air" and quoted in *Newsweek* magazine. Also featured in *Direct Marketing News*, and *U.S. News and World Report*.

National Public Radio
DIRECT MARKETING DIVISION HEAD
1997 - Present

- **Created a new direct marketing department**. Changed direct response agencies. Improved acquisition effectiveness more than 50%, and increased retention.
- Initiated acquisition investment models, subsequent value analyses, and retention benchmarks.
- Increased revenue by improved segmentation and targeted mailings.
- Selected to direct an $11 million product marketing business including catalog mail order, retail and volunteer consignment.

VICE PRESIDENT, SYSTEMS & OPERATIONS
1987 - 1997

- Directed a $3.6 million catalog mail order business, **increasing revenue to $6.5 million in 3 years**.
- In three months, turned around a troubled computer facility, and installed database software saving $250,000 annually.
- Built a stable and effective systems & operations department (35 staff) supporting an increase in direct mail revenue from $4.3 million to $14 million in seven years.
- Negotiated corporate grants from Digital Equipment Corporation to purchase over $1 million in computer equipment for half the retail price.
- Appointed acting Chief Financial Officer.

REPUBLICAN NATIONAL COMMITTEE
Director, Management Information Systems
1983 - 1987

- Prepared business plans and developed computer database support to increase direct mail revenue five-fold.
- Initiated, planned, and implemented a new direct marketing computer center reducing automation costs by $30,000 per month.
- Invited by IBM to address their President's Assembly on the effective use of IBM systems.

LIBRARY OF CONGRESS
Chief, Copyright Planning and Technical Office   1975 - 1983

- Planned and directed the complete automation of the U.S. Copyright Office of 600 staff including implementing widespread organizational and workflow changes.
- Reduced the time to process routine copyright claims from six the three weeks, while improving service.
- Appointed Acting Executive Officer.
- Received award for Outstanding Performance.

Previous Assignments

- In a single year, planned and implemented an on-line automated retrieval system to track the status of all legislation introduced in the <u>U.S. Congress</u>.
- Directed management information and business systems consulting, first in Amsterdam and then in London for Auerbach Associates, Inc.
- Managed programming and software development projects for IBM's Federal Systems Division.

EDUCATION

- Harvard Graduate School of Business, Executive Education Program
- Princeton University, B A. Mathematics

PROFESSIONAL RECOGNITION

- Invited to speak at numerous Direct Marketing conferences in the U.S. and Europe:
  Direct Marketing Association:
  > Annual Catalog Conference (Chicago - June 1997)
  > Annual Conference (Dallas - October 1997)
  > Non-Profit Conference (Washington, DC - January 1998)
  National Public Radio:
  > Direct Marketing Fundraising Seminars (1996 - 1998)
  > Paris, London, Madrid, and Geneva

PROFESSIONAL ASSOCIATIONS

- Direct Marketing Association:
  Board Member, Nonprofit Council Operating Committee
  Computer/Information Technology Council
- International Society for Information Management (SIM):
  Board of Directors and Executive Committee
  Past Chairman, Greater New York Chapter

The Five O'Clock Club®

PART FIVE

RÉSUMÉS FOR EXECUTIVES

Tom:
What Did He *Really* Do?

*We are challenged on every hand to work untiringly to
achieve excellence in our lifework. Not all men are
called to specialized or professional jobs; even fewer
rise to the heights of genius in the arts and sciences;
many are called to be laborers in factories, fields, and
streets. But no work is insignificant. All labor that
uplifts humanity has dignity and importance and
should be undertaken with painstaking excellence.
If a man is called to be a street sweeper, he should
sweep streets even as Michelangelo painted, or
Beethoven composed music, or Shakespeare wrote
poetry. He should sweep streets so well that all the
host of heaven and earth will pause to say, "Here lives
a great street sweeper who did his job well."*
Martin Luther King, Jr.

Tom Warren's old résumé is pretty standard:
he states the jobs he's had and what he did in
each one. It's the same old historical approach.
The problem is that his résumé leaves out all of
the important parts. For his new résumé, we simply
added four parts: the all-important summary and
three introductory paragraphs that state what Tom
really did in each job. (For the purposes of this
example, we have reproduced only the first page of
Tom's two-page résumé.)

For example, in the last job on the page of the
old résumé, he states that he managed eight Manhattan branches. We had already completed his
Seven Stories Exercise, so I knew there was more to
his personality than this implied. Here is how our
discussion went:

Kate: "Tom, do you want to manage bank
branches?"

Tom: "Not a chance. I hate branch management."

Kate: "But this résumé positions you, among other
things, as a branch manager."

Tom: "That's what I did in that job."

Kate (I try to provoke him): "But to me this sounds
so boring. What did you really do in that job?
What is it you brag to your wife that you did?"

Tom: "Kate, you don't understand. That job was
important. *I turned around the largest problem-
ridden branch business in the company.*"

Kate: "Oh, excuse me, Tom. How could I have
known? I don't see that on your résumé. Let's
put it on there. Now, what kinds of things
would you like to do next?"

Tom: "I want to build major businesses or turn
around problem brands."

Kate: "Have you done those things before?"

Tom: "Yes, I definitely have."

Kate: "Then let's put that in your summary. It will
dramatically increase your chances of getting
to do those things again. "

That's what you have to do too. For most
people, the problem is not that they stretch the truth
on their résumés; the problem is that they unwit-
tingly fail to tell the truth: they don't say what they
really did.

Figuring this out is much more difficult than
simply reciting your job description. That's why it's
important to do the Seven Stories Exercise (which
you will find in the front of this book and in our
book *Targeting the Job You Want*). It helps you step
back from a résumé frame-of-mind so you can
concentrate on the most important accomplishments of your life. Then the exercise helps you to
think about each accomplishment: what led up to it,
what your role was, what gave you satisfaction,
what your motivation was, and so on.

We added those parts to Tom's résumé and left
the rest alone. In fact, the parts we added are the
only parts that really matter—so those are highlighted and the rest becomes the background. Now
Tom has a good sales piece—one that truly reflects
what he did.

This new résumé is a *strategic document. It looks
ahead, not back.* It thinks about what he would like to
do next, and then finds those experiences in his
background that support what he wants to do. In
addition, it highlights those areas that were the
most satisfying. Now he has increased his chances
of finding a new job where he repeats or builds on
those satisfying experiences.

THOMAS WARREN

2343 Fifth Avenue   Home: 212-333-4444
New York, New York 11000   Business: 212-555-1111

PREMIERBANK   1987-Present

International Institutions Group   1996-Present
Director of Electronic Banking

Responsible for support and development of all interbank payment and information systems.

* Developed and market tested a new offline funds transfer product.
* Upgraded and repositioned existing worldwide online payment system.
* Created line-wide repricing plan to maximize target customer penetration.
* Developed strategy to integrate payment, information and securities products.

New York Retail Bank   1994-1995
Director, Special Marketing Group

Responsible for growth and profitability of the New York Bank's $13-Billion consumer portfolio.
Managed new product development, pricing and sales promotion.

* Developed, positioned and introduced the PremierBank Investment Portfolio,
     PremierBank's first mass-market integrated investment product. Created new
     portfolio-selling concept to incorporate it into the branch sales process.
* Established more efficient PremierBank core-account promotion tactics.
* Developed new investment savings product.
* Created unique research method to guide new product development.

Senior Area Director, Financial District   1994

Managed eight Manhattan branches with $31-million net revenue and $1.2-billion total footings.
Responsible for total branch performance including sales, service, control, revenue and expenses.

* Put new management team in place in three key branches.
* Reversed balance declines by revitalizing business-account marketing.
* Established distribution strategy and plan for World Trade Center marketplace,
     including customer and business offsites.
* Developed a high-net-worth tailored credit program for area with $2 million-$3 million
     annual revenue potential.
* Initiated regional staffing efficiency analysis, which significantly improved
     branch productivity.

THOMAS WARREN

2343 Fifth Avenue
New York, New York 11000

Home: 212-333-4444
Business: 212-555-1111

SUMMARY

Innovative financial-services marketer with ten years at PremierBank and heavy package-goods product-management experience. Created new products. Built major businesses. Turned around problem brands. Strong strategic thinker and team builder.

Areas of Expertise

o **Product Management**
o **New Product Development**
o **Sales Management**

o **Electronic Banking**
o **Branch Banking**
o **Market Analysis**

PREMIERBANK   1987-Present

International Institutions Group   1996-Present
Director of Electronic Banking

Created a multi-year business plan to restore PremierBank's leadership in interbank electronic payments through the worldwide rollout of superior offline payment products.

Responsible for support and development of all interbank payment and information systems.
* Developed and market tested a new offline funds-transfer product.
* Upgraded and repositioned existing worldwide online payment system.
* Created line-wide repricing plan to maximize target customer penetration.
* Developed strategy to integrate payment, information and securities products.

New York Retail Bank   1994-1995
Director, Special Marketing Group

Created the New York retail bank's first effective way to package and sell its diverse investment product line.

Responsible for growth and profitability of the New York Bank's $13-billion consumer portfolio. Managed new product development, pricing and sales promotion.
* Developed, positioned and introduced the PremierBank Investment Portfolio, PremierBank's first mass-market integrated investment product. Created new portfolio selling concept to incorporate it into the branch sales process.
* Established more efficient PremierBank core-account promotion tactics.
* Developed new investment-savings product.
* Created unique research method to guide new product development.

Senior Area Director, Financial District   1994

Reorganized and redirected a large, problem-ridden branch business to restore balance and revenue growth.

Managed eight Manhattan branches with $31-million net revenue and $1.2-billion total footings. Responsible for total branch performance including sales, service, control, revenue and expenses.

Donald: Repositioned into a New Industry

*In making our work a gift to the world, in making it
an expression of our love for life, for God, and for our
fellow man, we fulfill our highest potential,
our most beautiful destiny as human beings.*
Michael Lynberg, *The Path With Heart*

*Summing up her career in her autobiography, she
said: "My attitude had never changed. I cannot
imagine feeling lackadaisical about a performance.
I treat each encounter as a matter of life and death.
The one important thing I have learned over the years
is the difference between taking one's work seriously
and taking one's self seriously.
The first is imperative and the second disastrous."*
Dame Margot Fonteyn,
Obituary in *The New York Times*

**This résumé has served as
one of the most popular
examples for executives at
The Five O'Clock Club.**

Donald had become known as a guru in the record business, a relatively small industry. The chances of finding another position in that industry were slim, and even if they had not been, Donald was ready for a change. He had worked many years, expected to work many more, and so wanted to reposition himself—as someone who could work in different kinds of businesses. Therefore, his résumé *does not mention the industry in which he worked*. In addition, he got rid of *all* industry jargon including the names of the celebrities with whom he had worked. Except for the company names themselves, which he cannot change, a reader cannot tell that his experience was actually narrowly focused.

Before Donald went on interviews, he studied in-depth the industries of the people he approached—he came across as an insider. He was extremely knowledgeable in his conversations with senior management. He sounded so authoritative that it never became an issue that Donald had not worked in those industries.

The following résumé is on 3 pages. It has served as one of the most popular examples at The Five O'Clock Club and hundreds of clients have used this format for their own résumés. The front page of this résumé is a summary so that the reader cannot possibly see the specialty companies Donald worked for (on pages 2 and 3), but instead presents him as a marketing executive who can work for virtually any company.

On the other hand, if Donald had wanted to present himself as a specialist in the record industry, that specialty would have been in the headline of his summary. It's as easy as that.

By the way, Donald ended up with three concurrent offers—none in the record industry. He did an excellent job of developing his Personal Marketing Plan (see our book *Targeting Interviews*), and contacted *every* company on his target list. He always had six to ten things in the works, kept his spirits up, and served as a role model for other clients. He had private counseling sessions in addition to the group, and landed the right job within ten weeks.

Donald Garafalos
334 Lexington Blvd.
Mansfield, TX 00997
555.789.5448 (day) - garafalosxx@aol.com

Global Strategic Marketing Executive
with extensive Management Consulting experience

*Global expert with over 15 years of experience in domestic / international
business services, marketing strategies, and performance improvement.
Consistently successful in pursuing business growth in emerging markets.
Focused on top management strategy-related issues.*

Strategy Development   Market Assessment   Organizational Effectiveness

Brought cutting-edge technology solutions in strategy analysis to a $6 billion company:

- Assessed **38 offices around the world** and defined the **strategic business plan** for the company world-wide, including Europe, South East Asia and Latin America. Recommended informed solutions.
- **Maintained growth** by creating value, using networked-based "industry information clearinghouses."
- Developed a uniform and creative global approach for marketing issues and information technology critical to the **long-term competitiveness** of this industry.
- Contributed to moving the company **from #5 to #2** in its sector within 3 years.

Member of 5-person steering committee reporting directly to chairman:

- Oversaw **global implementation** of company priorities. **Traveled extensively** to all markets. Monitored progress, reviewed targets and reported back to the board on a **quarterly basis**.
- Supplemented **strong growth in North America** by even stronger results in **Europe** and truly exceptional performance in **Southeast Asia and Latin America**.

*Took a product that did not sell internationally and moved sales from 150,000 units
to 5 million within 18 months.*

- Motivated **hundreds of marketing executives** around the world.
- Helped company executives understand **electronic commerce** and the effect on the industry.
- Worked closely with TV networks, local governments, retail outlets to develop this brand into **household name**.

Managed budgets of $10 million plus; staff of 20:

- Created and staffed highly successful marketing and sales divisions at **major companies**.
- Quickly built **trust and credibility** with business associates.
- **Resolved issues** based on cultural differences.

*Resourceful problem solver, quickly identifying problems.
Recommend timely and effective solutions.*

Business Management Inc.   1997 till present

Increasing worldwide sales through targeted marketing.

- Implement marketing strategies market by market maximizing product sales in major countries.
- Build licensing teams around the world.
- Create distribution networks and seek opportunities in emerging markets.
- Monitor marketing activities at local level, acting quickly on resolving issues.

Maintain highly productive working relationships and provide a creative platform that enables our business associates to be a driving force in the global arena.
Help shape our clients global impact as well as to achieve long term profitability.

Bertlesman North America   1994-1997
Vice President Global Strategy and Communications, West Coast

Established company's division as a global leader in its field, making that division the most profitable business of the group with $10 million in annual international income.

- Directed company's marketing team in 64 countries achieving 40% sales increase.
- Traveled around the world leading priority projects.
- Oversaw multimillion dollar advertising budget.
- Member of company's executive committee, advising board on strategic international-related issues.

General Electric USA   1992-1994
Vice-President International, Amazon Records Group

Created the company's international marketing division: now the #1 profit center for the Group generating over $50 million in annual foreign income.

- Hired staff including senior sales positions; conducted sales and marketing training.
- Designed and implemented priority system and marketing planning procedures to optimize margins, market share, growth and volume and reduce operating costs.
- Created marketing strategies, understanding the needs and nuances of all cultures, producing extraordinary sales, capturing the full international potential.
- Managed advertising, promotion and sales initiatives, securing great deals.
- Introduced product development techniques, increasing sales through targeted marketing and producing brand identification for new lines.
- Introduced international artist development techniques, increasing sales through targeted marketing producing brand identification for new products and recorded goods.
- Consolidated reports including sales figures, competition performance and market share data for the chairman covering over 100 projects on a monthly basis.
- Demonstrated great fiscal responsibility while evaluating marketing budgets.

CBS / WORLDWIDE   1987-1992
Vice President, International, CBS Records Group, 1990-1992

Delivered 120% international sales increase and established CBS-USA as a major player around the world. Guided marketing, sales and promotion in 46 offices.

- Created and delivered high impact sales presentations motivating extraordinary performance by creative teams around the world. Produced 20 minute infomercials and electronic press kits.
- Guided quarterly strategy meetings on site in Europe, Asia and Latin America to focus on company-wide priority issues.
- Designed and implemented an International Product Release System that is marketing-driven and creatively-led, facilitating local manufacturing, streamlining operations and promoting corporate communications. This system enables a simultaneous global release schedule and prevents costly import of records by the local companies.
- Improved profitability by reducing departmental costs and monitoring marketing expenses.
- Represented the chairman effectively at international corporate events and conventions. Conducted acquisitions and identified viable business opportunities.

Director, International Marketing and Communications, CBS Worldwide   1987-1990
- Headed marketing and sales for the territories outside of North America and Europe.
- Increased South East Asia regional sales from 15% to 25% in one fiscal year.
- Directed international marketing efforts for North American properties, supervised staff of ten including the London office that was in charge of European Marketing.

Columbia Records   Paris and New York   1978-1987
Manager, International Promotion, Columbia Records New-York   1983-1987

- Handled all media communications for Columbia-US clients. Organized all global media events for the corporate affairs department.

International Label Manager, Columbia/Chrysalis France Paris   1978-1983

- Approved and scheduled all international releases originating from UK/US. Supervised marketing department for local products.

EDUCATION
Fluent in French and Spanish
UCLA - Legal course in Business Affairs (1997)
The EFAP school of Marketing and Public Relations (Paris - 1977)
Lycée Bergson, graduate (Paris-1978)

David:Handled His Fear of Discrimination

No spring nor summer beauty hath such grace,
As I have seen in one autumnal face.
John Donne, *The Autumnal*

At thirty, man suspects himself a fool;
Knows it at forty, and reforms his plan.
Edward Young

If man is to vanish from the earth, let him
vanish in the moment of creation,
when he is creating something new,
opening a path to the tomorrow he may never see.
It is man's nature to reach out,
to grasp for the tangible
on the way to the intangible.
Louis L'Amour, *The Lonesome Gods*

(The secret of how) to live without resentment or
embarrassment in a world in which I was different
from everyone else . . . was to be indifferent
to that difference.
Al Capp, "My Well-Balanced Life
on a Wooden Leg," *Life,* May 23, 1960

As long as you keep a person down, some part of you
has to be down there to hold him down, so it means
you cannot soar as you otherwise might.
Marian Anderson,
who sang at the Lincoln Memorial in 1939

David was worried that he would have difficulty finding a new position because he was an older man and lacked formal schooling. Yet, using the following résumé, he received four excellent offers within a very short time.

In creating the résumé, we concentrated on the assets; his strengths—properly stated—allowed us to position him effectively.

David has steadily advanced in his career. To those within his industry, every line on his résumé is impressive. In his summary, David notes how he is different from others in his field.

The résumé is compact and clear—eliminating any accomplishment that would be considered routine.

No one even noticed that David had not gone to college. What's more, no one could have accomplished what David had without having been around a few years. His age actually became an advantage.

Don't Be So Sure Your "Weakness" is Showing

Most job hunters have something that they think will keep them from getting their next job. It could be that they feel they are too young or too old, have too little education or too much, are of the wrong race, creed, nationality, sex or sexual orientation, weight or height, or are very aware that they have a physical disability.

While it is true that there is prejudice out there, job hunters who are too self-conscious about their perceived handicaps will hold themselves back.

In addition, they may inadvertently draw attention to their "problem" during the interview. Your attitude must be: "What problem? There is no problem. Let me tell you about the things I've done."

DAVID WALTERS

942 Cherry Hill Road
Los Angeles, CA 99125

Business: 222 555-3907
Home: 222 555-1074

SUMMARY OF QUALIFICATIONS

Treasury executive with over 20 years of international as well as domestic experience. Possess a clear understanding of the basic interrelationship of all aspects of the financial markets. At the forefront of simple, innovative solutions that are easily acceptable to others and later adopted at large. Record of generating new customer business. Lived and worked in many countries. Proficient in a number of languages. Strong turn-around and people-management skills.

EXPERIENCE

AMBANK, N.A.   **1974 - Present**

Individual Bank   1994 - Present
Vice President/Regional Treasurer
Middle East/Africa & Greece - Dubai

Established and controlled Treasury Units for the Individual Bank in Greece, Saudi Arabia, Oman, Bahrain and the U.A.E. to manage the risks of a portfolio totaling $3,200 billion.

- Set up Treasury function in 3 countries. Earned $2 million in 1988 ($1 million above budget).
- Developed a unique funding strategy that overcame local regulatory restrictions and reduced Ambank (Greece) borrowing costs by 5%.
- Developed a hedging strategy in highly restricted market. Avoided losses in excess of $1 million.
- Analyzed and identified the liquidity and interest-rate risks inherent in the business and developed and implemented a strategic plan to manage the risk.
- More than doubled foreign-exchange business in one year.

Investment Bank   1993 - 1994
Vice President/Treasurer - Panama

Created and managed a team of 7 professionals to control funding and liquidity of $350 million, managed foreign exchange, and observed regulatory constraints.

- Reorganized the treasury to address foreign-exchange needs. Expanded the marketing function.
- Increased corporate FX business tenfold in 14 months. Expanded FX into Central American currencies (Ambank became a "Market Maker" in Central American currencies).
- Installed an independent system to record Ambank's liquidity position in order to implement effective funding and reduce risk.
- Structured and implemented one of the first 3rd-party debt deals in Central America. Reduced El Salvador's debt at substantial savings. Ambank's first year intermediary fee exceeded $100 million.

100

Institutional Bank   1989 - 1993
Vice President/Training Center Administration Manager - Puerto Rico

Brought in to design and teach courses to develop Treasury in Latin America. Managed a team who coordinated all training-center courses.

- Developed treasury courses for all management levels. Consistently received high ratings.
- Managed a team of 4 administrators. Quickly turned a department in disarray with no budget controls into a smooth-running operation.
- Negotiated to reduce hotel costs 50%. Negotiated the construction of a classroom to Ambank specifications (which the hotel named the "Ambankgarden Room").
- Consulted with local management in Honduras and the Dominican Republic on new products and treasury services.

Vice President/Division Treasurer - Venezuela   1988 - 1989

Controlled the Treasury function in 4 countries (Venezuela, Aruba, Ecuador and Colombia). Assisted local management in developing and implementing a treasury strategy.

- To grow customer business, obtained permission from government authorities to engage in fiduciary business. This represents at least $2 million annual earnings, and is a major source of income.

Vice President/Cash and Currency Consultant - Hong Kong   1985 - 1986

Created and managed the cash- and currency-consulting function in Asia which was used by multinational customers as well as within Ambank.

- Consulted with approximately 50 multinational companies.
- Created 4 major new products which were successfully used in 8 countries.

International Money Market - New York   prior to 1985
Corporate Systems Advisory Unit Head

Managed a team of 5 consultants and 2 administrators to design Foreign Exchange Exposure reports and perform international cash-management studies for multinational companies.

- Created AMBANKDATA/AMBANKRATE, a currency data base which 15 years later is being actively used by corporate clients as well as in-house.
- Completed 10 Cash Management Studies.

HOECHST ETECO, S.A. - Ecuador   1972 - 1974

Managed the Chemical and Dyestuff Department, supervising 2 salesmen. Tripled sales in 15 months.

LANGUAGES

Fluent in Spanish and German. Familiar with Portuguese and Dutch.

OTHER ACTIVITIES

Regularly lecture on currency management and cash management issues including
two appearances at Sloan School/MIT.

Martin: Is a One-Page Résumé Better?

It is not praise that does me good,
but when men speak ill of me, then, with a noble
assurance I say to myself, as I smile at them,
"Let us be revenged by proving them to be liars."
Catherine II ("The Great"),
Empress of Russia

Who would not say that it is the essence of folly to do
lazily and rebelliously what has to be done . . . ?
Seneca

Many people think a one-page résumé is better because they think it is more likely to get read. But the average résumé is looked at for only ten seconds—regardless of length. The question is; what does the reader *see* in those ten seconds?

Martin's résumé proves that a short résumé is not necessarily better. His résumé was not presenting him the way he wanted to be presented. A lot of information forced into one unreadable page does not advance his cause. Besides, it is the typical historical résumé—focusing on the past. It states each job and describes what he did in each.

Martin had been searching for six months by the time I met him, but he had not managed to get any meetings with people at a level higher than his. He earned in excess of $200,000 and would be on payroll for another full year (lucky him), but he was very discouraged.

Take a look at Martin's old résumé. It is written in dense paragraphs with narrow margins and a small font. No one will read it! Yet he had taken such pains to get it all onto one page—because conventional wisdom has held that one-page résumés "get read."

Not only is it unreadable, it's unscannable. Remember: the reader has to get your message in only ten seconds. At the very least, the accomplishments should be bulleted to make them readable, and that alone will generally make the résumé longer than one page.

The old résumé has a summary, but it too is historical. For example, the second bullet brags that Martin moved a data processing facility from New York to New Jersey. The reader will probably think: "We don't need to have a data processing center moved." It's not a selling point to the majority of his readers—so let's not mention it.

What is Martin 's real message here? It's that he saved the company $1 million —so that's what we mention on the new résumé. We highlight those things the reader might be interested in, which Martin would like to do again. For example, he wanted to be positioned as a key member of the senior management team. This kind of thinking resulted in a strategic résumé.

Carefully study Martin 's résumé—before and after. Compare the old summary to the new one, and the write-up of each old job to the new write-up. It should give you a better feel for how you want to position yourself on *your* new résumé.

MARTIN G. BUDIANSKY

6 Cucumber Lane   Dorrisville, NJ 07000   (201) 555-6878

PROFILE

Senior Information Systems executive with significant record of accomplishments and experience in multiple industries, both domestic and international. An unbroken record of increasing responsibilities marked by measurable achievements in support of business growth and profitability objectives. Unique ability to successfully integrate and consolidate business functions into the mainstream organization. A successful leader and motivator of people who possesses the practical judgment to function successfully in centralized and decentralized business cultures. A consistent contributor to the attainment of business goals and maximizing operating efficiencies.

- Consolidated into a single order-processing, customer-service operation 4 distinct businesses totaling $270 million in sales; this yielded a net annual savings of $1.4 million and enabled the business units to achieve additional synergies.

- Saved $1 million annually by relocating an entire data processing organization from New York to New Jersey. Additional savings followed by the relocation of all support operations. This was accomplished without sacrifice to operating efficiency.

- Created and implemented international financial reporting system for 72 worldwide locations. Provided real time delivery of financial data; continuous cash-flow monitoring ongoing assessment of profitability and consolidation of all data to generate financial statements.

CAREER SUMMARY

Senior Vice President, MIS   HARCOURT & SIMON, INC.   1994-Present

Organize and direct a Management Information Systems group with a $16.5 million operating budget; responsible for 135 employees. Establish policies and strategic direction; manage development of application systems, operation of the corporate center and all telecommunications. Responsible for data processing activities at 23 remote locations; consolidated 11 of these into the central location. Personally developed strategic and tactical plans for integration and consolidation of all newly acquired businesses. Consolidated all systems for payroll, general ledger, accounts payable, inventory accounting and accounts receivable into centralized applications. Reduced the number of Central Processing Units at the corporate center from four to one.

Group Director, MIS   ESTÉE LAUDER INC.   1988-1994

Developed MIS strategies and budgets for seven domestic and seven international companies in the Health Care Division, while overseeing the fulfillment of those plans at 29 domestic and international data processing centers. Initiated and developed worldwide financial reporting system. Represented division on corporate steering committee.

Director, Information Systems and Services   ROHRER INC.   1981-1988

Directed all systems development, computer operations and telecommunications at the corporate center and three division data processing centers. Promoted to Director in 1980 after managing the activities of a six-day 24-hour computer operation (75-80). Established procedures for introduction of new application and system software. Reorganized departments to improve service and reduce the required number of personnel.

Systems Manager/Analyst   NJ BELL TELEPHONE COMPANY   1967-1981

Various inter-departmental assignments with heavy exposure to data processing and business systems development. Progressed from sales trainee to Manager, Business Systems.

EDUCATION

B.S. in Economics	Villanova University	1967
Advanced Studies (Executive Programs):	Duke University	1984
	Dartmouth College	1986

Martin G. Budiansky

6 Cucumber Lane
Dorrisville, N.J. 07000
201-555-6878

Senior Information Systems Executive

- Manufacturing
- Pharmaceuticals
- Health Services
- Consumer Goods
- Telecommunications
- Publishing

Key member of management team. Report directly to the COO or CEO.
Managed technological needs <u>for companies ranging from $250 million to over $1 billion.</u>

Rapidly Integrate/Consolidate Acquisitions/Businesses

- Consolidated the technologies and systems of <u>over $1 billion in acquisitions.</u>

- Consolidated <u>4 distinct businesses</u> totaling <u>$270 million</u> in sales into a single operation.
  - Net annual <u>savings of $1.4 million</u>.
  - Completely integrated within 8 months.
  - Enabled the business units to achieve significant additional savings.

- <u>Saved $1 million annually on $5 million</u> data processing budget
  — with no sacrifice to operating efficiency.

- Developed <u>composite information base</u>.
  - Helped management see company as a logical, manageable organization and find other market opportunities that fit in.
  - Company avoided the problems so often associated with multiple acquisitions.

- Created <u>international financial reporting system</u> for <u>73 locations worldwide.</u>
  - Real-time delivery of financial data.
  - Ongoing assessment of profitability.
  - Continuous cash-flow monitoring.
  - Consolidation of financial statements.

Key Member of Senior Management Team

- Use technology to <u>support and implement the strategic plans of the company</u>.
- Developed 3-year strategic plan. Presented to corporate Board of Directors.
- Sensitive to profitability and enhancement of investment.

Develop Systems That Support Today's Business Environment

- Telecommunications network for <u>32 locations;</u> <u>1400 terminals</u> online to mainframe.
- Quickly develop/introduce new systems: use the latest methodologies and techniques.
- Developed security and contingency back-up plans that <u>assure continuous operation</u>.

<u>A business manager and key member of the management team.
Use technology to achieve the strategic and profit plan of the organization
to allow companies to achieve a greater participation in their marketplace.</u>

Strong hands-on, project-oriented business manager, strategic planner and leader.
Successful in centralized and decentralized business cultures.
Manage and control major development projects.

SENIOR VICE PRESIDENT, MIS
HARCOURT & SIMON, INC. 1994-Present

Staff of 135. $16.5 million operating budget.

- As key member of senior management team
  —set policies and direction to support and **implement overall strategic goals of company**.
  —personally developed strategic and tactical plans for integration and **consolidation of all 39 newly acquired businesses**.

- **Developed methodology to quickly consolidate all companies** for payroll, general ledger, accounts payable, inventory accounting & accounts receivable into centralized applications.
  - **All went smoothly.** **No adverse impact** on any of the companies involved.
  - **Company saved $35 million.**

- Manage application development, computer operations and all telecommunications.
  - Also responsible for data processing at 23 remote locations. Consolidated 11 centrally.
  - Use the latest systems-development methodologies and techniques (Expert Systems, CASE technologies, CD-ROM).
    - For **quick development and introduction of new systems.**
    - **Helps company stay competitive and on top of a dynamically growing organization.**

- Closed 3 data processing centers with no adverse impact.
  - **Saved company $1 million annually on $5 million** data processing budget.

- **Developed management personnel** so they operated effectively and independently.

GROUP DIRECTOR
ESTÉE LAUDER, INC. 1988-1994

- Managed MIS plans, budgets & activities at **22 domestic and 7 international centers** (230 people).
- **Managed 7 domestic and 7 international companies.**
- Initiated and developed **world-wide financial reporting system**.
- Respresented division on corporate steering committee.

DIRECTOR, INFORMATION SYSTEMS AND SERVICES
ROHRER, INC. 1981-1988

Directed all systems development, computer operations and telecommunications at the **corporate center and 3 division data processing centers.**
- Established procedures for "problem-free" introduction of new application and system software.
- Improved service and reduced the required number of personnel.

SYSTEMS MANAGER/ANALYST
NJ BELL TELEPHONE COMPANY 1967-1981

Regularly promoted. Progressed from sales trainee to Manager, Business Systems.

EDUCATION

B.S., Economics, Villanova University, 1967
Executive Program, Duke University, 1984
Executive Program, Dartmouth College, 1986

Norman:
"Hiding" His Most Recent Job

How long must I wrestle with my thoughts and every
*   day have sorrow in my heart?*
How long will my enemy triumph over me?
. . . But I trust in your unfailing love; my heart
*   rejoices in your salvation.*
I will sing to the Lord, for he has been good to me.
            Psalm, Old Testament

Life has got to be lived—that's all there is to it.
At 70 I would say the advantage is that you take life
more calmly. You know that "This too shall pass!"
            Eleanor Roosevelt

Yes, Virginia, there is a Santa Claus.
New York Sun editorial, 1897

Norman called me in distress from California. He was not proud of his performance in the last three years, and felt that he had failed. He wanted a résumé that would exclude that time.

We did the entire project over the phone. It took about six hours total to talk about his situation and background, and complete the résumé—which did *not* hide what he had done during the past three years.

Most of the people I work with have had great careers—until just a little while before I meet them. That's why they are calling me. Things are negative. They want to move on, and are not sure how to position their present situation.

In Norman's case, my business background came in handy. He told me what had happened during the past three years. The way he described it, it seemed terrible. After taking many notes, I noticed the positives. Often, ambitious people do not fulfill the goals they had in mind, and thus consider themselves failures. They discount everything that they have done—even the positives. Yet, a person has often done something worthwhile, has learned much from a failing situation, and can market that experience. It simply requires a different spin.

I said to him, "Norman, here's what it sounds

like to me: You did a great job growing the company, but it ran a bit ahead of your working capital. When you realized this, you hustled around to find someone to conduct a friendly takeover of the firm. These people liked and respected you so well that they wanted to keep you on to run that company and another company of theirs as well. Is that right?"

Norman couldn't believe his ears. "Everything you said is true! But I haven't been looking at it that way." Later, he said, "For three years, I've been very depressed. Now I feel like a new person."

Many of you may be in a similar situation. You are glum. Perhaps it looks as if you have done a bad job. Maybe you have. But chances are, there is a good explanation for what happened. If you can get some distance and look at it with new eyes, you may be on the road to resolving the predicament you are now in.

Norman's résumé is a good example of many of the things I preach. First of all, he did the Seven Stories Exercise so it would become clear which parts we should highlight. The stories gave a good overview of his career—what he was good at and what he was proud of.

Norman originally wanted two résumés: one he could use in the fashion industry, where he had spent his working life; and another in case he had to look outside the industry, given its present condition. Actually, as so often happens, one résumé served both purposes.

Now let's take a look at Norman's résumé in detail. . .

Norman's summary positions him as a person who grows profitable businesses. This is in stark contrast to his old résumé, which made him look like a manufacturing expert.

In real life, Norman's résumé is on one piece of paper (17" across x 11" down) folded—so it comes out 8.5" x 11". It's four pages long, but it looks like a booklet. The summary appears on the front. Page 2 appears on the inside left, page 3 on the inside right, and page 4 on the back.

"Hiding" Three Years

Page 2 contains the years he wanted to hide. If we had had a shorter summary on page 1, part of this time-frame would have appeared on page 1, and that would not have been good. Another strategy would have been to cut this part very short.

But I felt Norman had a lot to brag about during those years, and I didn't want to short-change him. The most important story in his résumé is on page 3. Therefore, page 2 contains a lot of information. It contains so much that the reader's eye tends to skip right across to page 3. The second page was made crowded intentionally.

Highlighting the Main Story

On page 2, the word PRESIDENT is meant to stand out before the reader's eye goes on to page 3. On page 3, the story is that Norman started this company. The main message runs down the center of the page: Took the Company from 0 to $13 million . . . from Business Start-up . . . and Financing . . . to Business Development . . . and the running of Day-to-Day Operations. That's the main message.

There are subordinate messages too. For example, under Business Start-up, the subordinate message is "Hired all key sales . . . " This message is underlined because it is so important, yet it does not detract from the main message. There are other subordinate messages. For example, under Financing, the words "creative financing techniques" are highlighted—but not enough to detract from the main message. Under Business Development the subordinate message is "7,500 women at the Republican National Convention." And under the last section, the subordinate message is "skilled negotiator."

Full of Inconsistencies

Now take a look at all the job titles and company names. On page 2, the first job has no title at all. That's because the job title there would have detracted from the main message, which is that Norman runs entire companies. The word "president" in the middle of that page is highlighted. At the top of page 2, the company name is underlined and bolded. The company name at the middle of the page, however, is neither underlined nor bolded, to deemphasize it.

On page 3, the company name is in caps because this company name is prestigious (the real one, that is—this one is fictitious). On the back page, the job title that sticks out most is "president." The other company names or job titles are highlighted as appropriate.

I can assure you that no one asks why a certain title or company name is highlighted. It's obvious why. And it isn't offensive, is it?

Various but Appropriate Formats

There is a further inconsistency in this résumé. It has four pages, and each one is in a *completely different format*. Each page is formatted in a way that is appropriate for the message we are trying to convey on that page. The summary is very different from page 2, which is different from page 3. The back page approaches a more normal résumé format, but there are still inconsistencies in the titles and company names.

We are trying to tell a story. And we use the format that does this best. No one looks at this résumé and notices that there are four different formats.

Our Main Goal: Get the Message Across

Decide what message you are trying to tell. Does your story pop out? Or do you simply record your history and leave it up to the reader to figure out its significance? That's not good enough! It is your job to decide how you want to position yourself, and then go to the trouble of doing it.

The result is a résumé that speaks for you, and interviews where people tend to ask you about the parts you want to emphasize.

There's no reason to have your present negative situation color the entire rest of your background. The résumé proudly presents your experience so that the reader recognizes your accomplishments and your potential within the marketplace.

Norman S. Neumann

5341 Churchcross Road
Los Angeles, California 90074
213-555-7220
213-555-0876 (message)

Summary of Qualifications

Senior General Management Executive with over 20 years of P&L and functional management experience. Consistently **grow profitable businesses from 0 to millions in a short time frame**.

Areas of Expertise include:

- **Overall Business Management**
- **Start-up Operations**
- **Financing**
- **New Business Development**
- **Sales and Marketing Management**
- **Manufacturing and Operations Management**
- **Merchandising and Cost Control**
- **Management/Planning/Restructuring**
- **Negotiations with Landlords, Labor Unions and Vendors**

- A strong **start-up manager**. A troubleshooter and problem-solver. Successfully open up new companies. Expert in situations requiring high growth.

- Know every area of the business operations and the products down to the details.

- **Attract top-level sales and management teams on a national level.**

- Well-known, respected, and trusted in the industry as a top-of-the-table negotiator.

- **Strong working relationships at all levels in national chain and specialty stores** such as Neiman Marcus, Saks Fifth Avenue, Bergdorf Goodman, Lord & Taylor, I. Magnin & Company, Bullocks Wilshire, Robinsons, and Martha.

- Motivate executives as well as store personnel to back products and **insure success**.

- **Strong public image**. Inspire a high level of confidence.

- Strong presentation skills: to 7,500 women at the Republican National Convention, formal fashion shows for Saks and Neiman Marcus, and TV talk-show appearances.

- Highly experienced and successful in putting together National Co-op Advertising Programs in publications such as *Harper's, Vogue, W, Town and Country*, and *Connoisseur*.

- Senior-level experience in working with **Japanese-owned companies**.

A business-builder: able to produce high-quality merchandise, motivate a sales force, and develop long-term relationships with national chains and specialty stores of the highest quality.

Outgoing, friendly, intense, ambitious, well-traveled, straightforward "people-person."

Wearmagic, Inc.   1998-present

Manage two divisions: one start-up division and one turnaround of a problem division.

- **Reorganized and redirected a problem business** (R.L. Meyer Division).
  - Restored balance and revenue growth.
  - Now a $4-million business. Projected revenues of $6 million for 1999.

- In November, 1996, **developed and introduced the Koki Selman label**, a high-priced designer line of ladies' suits, costumes and dresses.
  - Project growth **from 0 to $3 million within first 12 months**.
  - Achieved **national product exposure** for Koki Selman **at a very low cost**. In catalogs such as Bergdorf's, Montaldo's, Talbot's, I. Magnin, and Neiman Marcus.
  - Implemented cooperative advertising programs.
  - **One of the top five showrooms in America**.

PRESIDENT   1996-1998
R.L. Meyer, Inc. (Later acquired by Wearmagic, Inc.)

Joined company in mid-1996, after it had loss for fiscal year just ended of $1.3 million sales. Company had antiquated plant and equipment, no equity, and a work force of 42—primarily workers on social security. **Immediately developed and implemented plan to turn around performance:**

- Strengthened financial and operating controls;
- **Negotiated favorable terms with a national factor and a substantially larger banking line of credit**;
- Revamped product line; To control costs, reorganized production operations;
- Increased prices by 30 to 40% to reflect actual costs that had never been analyzed;
- Started a sales force where none previously existed. Established sales organizations in New York, Chicago and Los Angeles;
- Broadened distribution and **increased sales to $6 million within one year**;
- **Negotiated major labor contract concessions;**
- Attracted large national catalogs and retail operations such as Talbot's, I. Magnin, Neiman Marcus, Saks Fifth Avenue, Bergdorf Goodman, Nordstrom.

As a consequence, sales increased dramatically. To attract the necessary long-term capital to support increased business, took the following actions:

- Initiated discussions with prospective equity partners.
- Took advantage of legal reorganization provisions.
- Developed a workable plan for reorganization and found purchasers for a friendly takeover.

Company became and is now a division of Wearmagic, Inc. Became responsible for:

- the continued growth of R. L. Meyer, and
- the start-up of another, now highly successful, division.

Stockholder/Vice President/Secretary   1988-1996

JORDAN HANES, INC.

Founded company with Jordan Hanes, designer. Established an exclusive manufacturing business of fine women's apparel. Collection of day and evening wear retailing from $250 to $1600.

Took the Company from 0 to $13 million, giving it a national reputation for quality and leadership.

Managed the entire business side of the company from:

Business Start-up . . .

- Established company from its inception: Procured leases, all necessary business licenses, Dun's number, and listing with Dun & Bradstreet.
- Organized, contracted and executed construction of facilities including all project management, and negotiation of budgeting and costing with all manufacturing contractors.
- **Hired all key sales and management personnel. All are still in place today.**

and Financing . . .

- Built a solid financial reputation on a national and international level.
- Used **creative financing techniques** to obtain favorable financing during start-up as well as during extraordinary growth. Received backing of national commercial factors.
- Secured lease in prime area of L.A. for only one-third of market rate.
- Through financing, increased capitalization by 40%; this increased profits by 10%.

to Business Development . . .

- Established and maintained a customer base of 803 active accounts including: Neiman Marcus, Saks Fifth Avenue, Bergdorf Goodman, Lord & Taylor, I. Magnin, Bullocks Wilshire, Robinsons, Martha.
- Staged 150-200 fashion shows, seminars and charity events including shows for the finest stores in America, and for **7500 women at the Republican National Convention**.
- Ran national clinics, fashion shows and trunk shows.
- Handled all advertising and promotional functions; negotiated and contracted with media/publcations.

and the running of all Day-to-Day Operations.

- Created, planned and implemented company fringe-benefit plan. Worked with corporate attorneys and accountants. Obtained government approval of pension and profit-sharing plans and tax-effective benefits for employees as well as executives.
- A **skilled negotiator** with vendors, suppliers and leasing companies. Obtained the lowest available cost while maintaining quality.
- Installed efficient administrative systems and controls that are still being used today.
- Set up and oversaw an efficient manufacturing production system that insured quality-control inspection and scheduling.
- Developed all procedure manuals and administrative responsibilities, shipping/ receiving, importing and inventory control.

Key Account Sales Consultant   1985-1988
Young Stuff, Incorporated

- **Starting with a territory of 0, developed sales into $6 million**, which accounted for 1/3 of total company billing.

La Milagros Cordero, a **national sales organization**   1984-1985

- A start-up operation.
- With partner, grew company **from 0 to $20 million**, sales offfices in New York and Los Angeles, and 11 salesmen.
- Negotiated exclusive rights to market in the U.S. and Mexico. Upscale, high-quality Spanish merchandise which included the finest-quality leather and suedes.

PRESIDENT   1978-1984
Mr. Chris for Men (high-quality men's clothing and furnishings)

- Company had been heavily in debt. **Within one year**:
  - removed all debt,
  - increased volume 120%
  - and square footage by 100%.

- **Made company highly profitable** with a volume of $4 million and 3 locations.
  - Made company cash-heavy and financially secure.
  - Received backing of national and local factors.
  - Through bank, negotiated substantial and favorable SBA loan for capital improvements.

- **Negotiated lease(s):**
  - that are still in place today and are producing substantial revenues.
  - with largest shopping center in America.
  - with major motion picture studio's real estate division.

Direct Sales Agent   1974-1978
John Rose California

- Assigned the company's smallest territory.
- **Starting from virtually 0, increased sales to over $3 million**.
- This accounted for **50% of the company's total sales**.

EDUCATION

B.S., Business Administration, The University of Southern California
Graduate, General Studies, The Mercersberg Academy

Janet: Changing Her Job Title; Downplaying Too Many Jobs

We act as though comfort and luxury were the chief requirements of life, when all we need to make us happy is something to be enthusiastic about.
Charles Kingsley

Understanding is a wellspring of life to him that hath it.
Proverbs

Janet was tired of telling people that she was more than a lawyer. Her title was Corporate Counsel, but her other responsibilities were more important.

After much probing, we discovered that the ideal next job for Janet would be Chief Financial and Administrative Officer in a medium-sized firm—exactly what she was currently doing.

With clients, I sometimes feel like Perry Mason in court. Here is a shortened version of our discussion:

Kate: "Janet, you are having trouble with your job search because you list Corporate Counsel as your job title, and that is how people see you. You keep trying to convince people that you were actually doing something else. But if you call yourself Corporate Counsel on your résumé, you are creating a handicap for yourself."

Janet: "That was my title, but if people read my résumé very closely, they will see that I also handled all financial and administrative matters for the company."

Kate: "People won't read your résumé very closely. Your résumé is a marketing piece, not a legal document. Could we truthfully say that you were the Chief Financial Officer for the company?"

Janet: "That wasn't my title."

Kate: "Was there anyone else in the company who could have been called the Chief Financial Officer?"

Janet: "No. I was it."

Kate: "If I had called your company and asked for the Chief Financial Officer, who would I have gotten?"

Janet: "You would have gotten me."

Kate: "Then, in fact, you were the company's Chief Financial Officer?"

Janet: "Yes. But that wasn't my title."

Kate: "Can you see that you are misleading the reader when you call yourself Corporate Counsel when you were in fact the company's Chief Financial Officer? And can you see that **we want to put on your résumé a job title that honestly reflects the actual job you were doing**—rather than some title they happened to give you? And can you also see that you will *not* get a job as a Chief Financial Officer if you insist on describing your function as Corporate Counsel?"

Janet: "I can see that."

Kate: "Is it true that you were responsible for all administrative matters in the company, such as personnel, computers, and so on?"

Janet: "Yes. That's true."

Kate: "Is it also true that you were the Chief Financial as well as the Chief Administrative Officer for the firm, in addition to being Counsel?"

Janet: "That's true."

Kate: "Would it be <u>in</u>accurate if we listed your job title as Chief Financial and Administrative Officer?"

Janet: "No."

Kate: **"Listing that as your job title would not only be more accurate, but it would also increase your chances of being viewed that way by the reader.** And that would increase your chances of getting another job doing that same thing. So, let's write it up this way and see how you do in your search with this changed positioning."

Janet: "Okay! Let's go for it."

When you do your résumé, think about the kind of job you want next, and then search your background to find things that support the direction you want to take. In Janet's résumé, we played down her legal background, and played up the financial and administrative experiences.

Janet had another problem: she had had a lot of different jobs. You'll notice, at the bottom of page three, how we list four jobs in such a way that the number is deemphasized.

By the way, Janet's résumé is on a 17" x 11" sheet folded so page 1 is on the front, pages 2 and 3 are inside and 4 is on the back.

112

© 1999, The Five O'Clock Club®, Inc.

JANET H. FUDYMA

2 Grove Street
Philadelphia, PA 19109

Office: (215) 554-2345
Home: (215) 556-1234

SUMMARY

Senior-level executive with broad-based management background. Experienced in corporate, legal and financial matters, human resources, strategic planning and regulatory affairs. Strong emphasis on analyzing and exploiting business opportunities and resolving business problems.

EXPERIENCE

CHICO-LAY U.S.A. INC.   **1995-PRESENT**
Vice President/Corporate Counsel

Vice President/Corporate Counsel for $80-million affiliate of leading multi-national food and beverage products company. Corporate officer with primary responsibility for corporate, legal, financial, treasury, human resources and quality control/quality assurance matters.

- Member of Senior management team responsible for establishing brand cost, pricing and promotional strategies.

- Innovated promotion authorization structure resulting in more accurate forecasting and customer profitability analysis while reducing improper deductions.

- Restructured benefits program to tailor coverage to specific needs of work force, thereby increasing employee morale while decreasing overall benefits costs.

- Restructured credit and accounts payable departments, dramatically increasing operating efficiencies and resulting in significant cash-flow benefits.

- Established Quality Control departments and directed implementation of Q.C. processes within production, warehousing and distribution functions, resulted in decreased scrap and costs associated with improper product handling and rotation.

- Successfully defended numerous advertising claims and challenged those of competitors, allowing company to continue aggressive thrust of products comparisons, while forcing competitors to retreat from focal issues of their campaign.

- Significantly curtailed rapidly growing trend toward illegal imports of company products by instituting landmark lawsuit against gray importers.

- Developed comprehensive emergency product recall procedures designed to ensure rapid and coordinated actions to minimize company losses and maintain consumer brand loyalty.

- Instituted consumer communication program which drastically reduced response time in addressing consumer inquiries, resulting in increased consumer satisfaction and improved relations with customers and brokers.

DAVIS & ASSOCIATES INC.   **1993-1995**
Vice President and Head of Midwest office of Financial and
Management Consulting firm, Engagements included client firms in construction,
manufacturing, service, communication and retail sectors.

- Opened new office in highly competitve environment and successfully established company reputation for quality and professionalism.

JANET FUDYMA

2 Grove Street
Philadelphia, PA 19109
Residence: 215-556-1234
Business: 215-554-2345

SUMMARY OF QUALIFICATIONS

Chief Financial and Chief Administrative Officer
Corporate Counsel

Manage all areas of corporate, financial and legal matters, strategic planning, regulatory affairs, human resources and quality control.

Areas of Expertise include:

- **Overall Business Management**
- **Financing**
- **Financial, Business & Production Controls**
- **Management/Planning/Restructuring**
- **Developing Management Personnel**
- **Strategic Planning**
- **Negotiating Skills**
- **New Business Development**

- Served as CFO for **entrepreneurially-driven $80 million company**.

- Actively involved in all aspects of running company.

- Provide financial and administrative support to high-growth situations:
    - Expert trouble-shooter and problem-solver.
    - Generate operating efficiencies and productivity improvements.

- A **skilled negotiator**: from dealings with vendors and suppliers to complex contracts and legal matters.

- Develop and motivate staff and management team.

- Strong **support to the sales and marketing** functions:
    - With CEO and VP of Operations, established all brand cost, pricing and promotional strategies.
    - Set all marketing, advertising and promotional budgets.
    - Approved all brand and product communication, labeling, copy and packaging.

A business manager who focuses on profits in growth situations.
Strong strategic vision coupled with overall business sense.
Able to translate strategic vision into workable organizational game plan.

Personable, pragmatic and analytical.
A straightforward, people-person conversant in many disciplines.
Brings order out of chaos.

CHIEF FINANCIAL AND ADMINISTRATIVE OFFICER
CORPORATE COUNSEL
Chico-Lay USA, Incorporated

1995-Present

Member of Senior management team running this $80 million company.

Corporate officer with primary responsibility for all corporate, financial and legal matters, strategic planning, regulatory affairs, human resources and quality control. Actively involved in all aspects of running the company.

- Designed and implemented **system for structuring deals**:
  - Analyzed account profitability.
  - Improved sales forecasting.
  - Reduced improper customer deductions.

- Managed **all financial and administrative areas:**
  - Took credit and A/R departments that were in disarray and turned them around.
    - **Dramatically improved cashflow.**
    - Significantly **increased operating efficiencies**.
  - Completely **restructured benefits program**.
    - Decreased overall benefit costs.
    - Increased employee morale.

- Established **Quality Control/Quality Assurance** department:
  - **Decreased** manufacturing **costs**.
  - Developed comprehensive **emergency product recall procedures**:
    - To minimize company losses.
    - To maintain consumer brand loyalty.
  - **Managed Consumer Affairs** function:
    - Drastically reduced response time.
    - Improved relations with customers and brokers.

- As **Corporate Counsel**:
  - **Initiated a landmark lawsuit to curtail illegal gray market imports.**
  - **Forced major competitor to retreat** . . .
    - . . . from overly aggressive trade advertising.

VICE PRESIDENT and HEAD OF CHICAGO OFFICE   1993-1995
Davis & Associates Incorporated
(Financial and Management Consulting Firm)

*Engagements included client firms in construction, manufacturing,
service, retail and communications sectors.*

- Opened new office in highly competitive environment.

- Successfully established company reputation for quality and professionalism.

- Arranged and brokered <u>**$40 million in financing and contracts**</u>
  on behalf of clients.

- Developed <u>**innovative compensation system.**</u>

  - Yielded increased productivity and employee morale.

- Served as <u>**chief spokesperson**</u> for company.

  - Appeared on panels, TV and radio.
  - Increased company visibility.

- Designed <u>**programs to win new clients**</u>.

  - Developed and delivered series of seminars.
  - Resulted in <u>**10% increase in client base**</u>.

KODAK/MGM PICTURES   1991-1993

*Manager of Financial Analysis—
for nation's largest videotape duplicator.*

- <u>**Troubleshooter for cost overruns and program delays.**</u>

- <u>**Headed**</u> finance department <u>**group responsible for**</u> financial analysis of <u>**special project.**</u>

- Responsible for <u>**capital appropriation studies**</u> and <u>**customer/product profitability analysis.**</u>

- Directed corporate treasury activities.

> Janet had four jobs in a short time, but see how formatting made these four jobs appear as one on her résumé.

Dobbs, Johnson, McLaughlin & Petersen   1989-1990
- <u>**Associate attorney**</u> with law firm specializing in tax-related matters.

Bucks County Health Department   1987-1989
- <u>**Fiscal Officer**</u> with primary responsibility for all financial and budgetary matters.

Burke Enterprises Incorporated   1983-1987
- <u>**Controller**</u> for chain of restaurants and night clubs.

EDUCATION

Kellogg Graduate School of Management, Northwestern University, 1994-1995
J.D., Thomas M. Cooley Law School, 1988
M.B.A., (Management), Central Michigan University, 1985
B.S. (Accounting), Penn State University, 1982

PROFESSIONAL LICENSES

Admitted to Bar:

State of Pennsylvania - February, 1989
State of Illinois - December, 1989

PROFESSIONAL AFFILIATIONS

Planning Forum
American Bar Association
Pennsylvania State Bar Association
American Corporate Counsel Association

The Five O'Clock Club®

PART SIX

RÉSUMÉS FOR MANAGERS AND HIGH-LEVEL PROFESSIONALS

Jessie: Pulling Together Her Background to Move Up

There is at bottom only one problem in the world and this is its name. How does one break through? How does one get into the open? How does one burst the cocoon and become a butterfly?
Thomas Mann, *Doctor Faustus*

I fall, I stand still . . . I trudge on, I gain a little . . . I get more eager and climb higher and begin to see the widening horizon. Every struggle is a victory.
Helen Keller,
on her studies at Radcliff College

Jessie's background is in marketing, customer service and training. She had also done a lot of work in database administration, but she didn't want to do *that* again.

When Jessie had done her Forty-Year Vision (see our book *Targeting the Job You Want*), she discovered that she wanted to have her own training company someday. She also thought she'd like to have four or five people working for her.

To head in that direction, it would be best if Jessie could work for a training consulting company (rather than in a corporate training department) and learn how the consulting firm ran its business. For example, she could learn how the firm marketed itself, priced services, administered programs and so on. Jessie thought it would be best if she not only did stand-up training for the firm, but also managed a few projects.

Jessie needed to decide what to write at the top of her résumé to position herself for the job she wanted next. You are most strongly positioned when you can say that you already *are* exactly what you want to do next. Since Jessie had already done training and project management, she highlighted those two skills at the top of her résumé. This increased the chance that hiring managers would want her to do exactly that for them. Since Jessie was also willing to market training programs, she highlighted her marketing skills as well.

When Jessie made up her list of target companies to contact in her search, she focused exclusively on training firms. She listed all the companies she could find in the training industry and called each one to find out the names of the people she should contact at each firm. (This can also be done by visiting Web sites.) She sent this résumé to each person with a cover letter, and followed up with phone calls (see our book, *Getting Interviews*).

Jessie got lots of meetings and landed long-term assignments with three consulting firms. She got to see how three different firms operated! The pay was excellent, by the way, and far exceeded what she had made in her corporate job. And she was learning how to run her own business when she was ready.

JESSIE WOODWARD

3010 Norwood Lane
Mansfield, Texas 55222

(555) 826-3555 (Home)
(555) 622-5800 (Office)

Training Manager / Project Manager
- Administration • Product Marketing

- **Coordinated 36 consultants and 200 executive seminars per year.**
  - In the course of four years, a class was never canceled due to mis-scheduling.
- Key player in design and implementation of a "Self-Directed Team," five-day training program.
- **Delivered a three-month training program. Designed curriculum.**
- Key player in $1 million dollar renovation of a four-story training facility.
- **Marketed training programs and materials.**
- Regularly taught a thirteen-day training program.
  - **Trained 25 students on bank procedures and computer systems.**
  - **Managed computer setup, testing, and troubleshooting.**
- Created a training guide for instructors to utilize during a thirteen day program.
- Content knowledge includes: Organization Vision & Values, Professional Image, Management Essentials, Customer Service / Sales Techniques, Retail/Wholesale Product Knowledge, Employee Benefits.

*Dynamic, goal-oriented, enthusiastic manager
with "outstanding interpersonal skills."*

InterFirst Bank, N.A.   1993 - present
Operations / Customer Service Manager

Administration / Negotiation / Information Systems

Marketing / Customer Service
- **Managed a customer service team of four direct reports.**
  - Conducted coaching sessions and performance reviews.
- Established goals and objectives.
- **Opened an average of 15 new accounts per quarter.**
- Maintained a standard of exceptional service for 200 middle market business customers.
  - Praised by customers for anticipating their needs and communicating effectively.

Information Systems / Administration
- Maintained a database of credit facilities over $80 million dollars.
  - **Provided ongoing training to the staff on system upgrades.**
- Maintained a tracking system for account activity.
- **Successfully negotiated past due loan payments in excess of $125 thousand.**
- Generated monthly document exception reports.
- Approved/processed money transfers, bankers acceptances and letters of credit.

Training Officer / Project Manager
- Performed needs analyses and actions plans as the organization moved forward.
  - Met with division executives to determine training goals and objectives.
  - Developed training curriculum and calendar.
- Provided training and coaching in the area of branch operations and sales techniques.
  - **Recognized as a seasoned trainer by top management.**

121

InterFirst Bank, N.A. , contd.   1993 - present
Training Officer / Project Manager, contd.

- Researched vendor services and negotiated contracts.
    - Managed a $250,000 expense budget.
- Facilitated "train-the-trainer" sessions.
- Interviewed and recruited retail bank staff.
- Managed the production of a training video.
- Maintained inventory of training material.

Training Manager / Administrator / Project Manager
- Managed an annual expense budget of $1 million dollars.
- Coordinated multiple executive-level seminars. Consistently praised for quality.
- Negotiated contracts with vendors and outside training facilities.
- Interfaced with domestic and international consultants on program design.
- Purchased office equipment. Organized training sessions.
- Managed the reorganization of a training library.

Dean Witter Reynolds   1988 - 1993
Sales Assistant
- Communicated products to high profile customers.
- Assisted a senior vice president with daily sales. Opened new accounts.
- Researched companies, annual reports, Standard & Poors ratings, etc.

Cashier Training Institute   1987 - 1988
Trainer
- Delivered multiple programs on a daily basis to a typical group size of 25 participants.
- Provided training on retail bank procedures, computer systems and secretarial techniques.
- Monitored participants' performance over a three-month time span.

Manufacturers Hanover Trust Company   1983 - 1986
Trainer / Operations Supervisor
- Supervised branch staff.
- Cross-sold products and opened accounts.
- Provided training in the areas of:
    - Customer Service   -   Computer Systems
    - Sales Techniques   -   Branch Procedures

EDUCATION

University of Dallas - Graduated 1991, School of Industrial and Labor Relations
University of Texas, Arlington - Business Administration Degree expected June 2002

AFFILIATIONS

Texas State Mentoring Program

Harold: In a Government Job; Aiming for a Promotion

A person working for the government who wants another government job has to be low-key in stating his accomplishments. He can't brag, for example, about the famous criminals he has captured.

However, the following résumé lists Harold's extensive Certifications and Commendations, which take all of page 3, followed by all of his Specialized Training and Courses, which take another page, followed by his education and then outside activities that show he was a good citizen (Cubmaster, etc.). It is easy to see that he has always been an outstanding performer. In addition, Harold thought it was important to include the personal information at the end of his résumé. Since he had not yet met some of the people who would decide about the promotion, he wanted them to know about his stable family situation, as well as his physical size—given the kind of work he did.

You can see how Harold understated his accomplishments. Do not worry about the résumé length. It was necessary to take this many pages to present the information in a readable way. For example, if he had squeezed his basic career history onto one page, it would have been unreadable. The material was presented on high-quality ivory stock, stapled in the upper left-hand corner. Harold came across as someone who cared—someone who did more, tried to learn more and was recognized throughout his career.

By the way, Harold's résumé helped him get the major promotion he wanted. There were many competitors for the job, but none had Harold's credentials—and it is safe to assume that no one presented his or her credentials as well as Harold did.

Harold R. Greenberg

15 Haverbrook Drive
Cash-in-Hand, NV 14555

Summary of Qualifications

Career State Investigator having 19 years experience;
over 14 years with the Division of Criminal Justice.

Extended diversified exposure both conducting and supervising investigation into the areas of economic crime, organized crime, and official corruption.

Since 1987, was a Division Instructor and representative to groups interested in the subject of various types of finance-related crime, its detection, investigation, and prosecution.

Professional Experience

Nevada Division of Criminal Justice, 1983-present
Office of the Attorney General

SUPERVISING STATE INVESTIGATOR OF THE ORGANIZED CRIME AND RACKETEERING BUREAU

1997-present

Conduct both financial and nonfinancial investigations of allegations concerning organized crime and official corruption.

Special Prosecutions Section

1992-1997

➤ Assigned to this section to investigate allegations of organized crime and official corruption.

➤ Specialized in financial implications.

➤ Investigations conducted for most part with Nevada State Police and allied agencies.

Major Fraud Unit
Senior State Investigator
State Investigator

1985-1992

➤ Conducted primarily finance-related investigations.

➤ Investigations involved areas such as:
- bank fraud and embezzlements,
- securities fraud (stocks, bonds, commodities and other investment schemes),
- insurance fraud (including reinsurance fraud),
- taxation frauds (including income taxation),
- sales and use tax,

Major Fraud Unit, contd.

➤ Areas involved, contd.:

- excise taxes (such as, motor fuels and employment taxes),
- unemployment fraud conspiracies, and
- other various schemes and offenses.

➤ Conducted investigation on individual and supervisory basis with
Division personnel, and with allied governmental agencies as necessary.

Nevada State Law Enforcement Planning Agency-   1982-1985
Executive Office of the Governor

Audit Supervisor
Auditor

➤ Established audit procedures and audit programs.

➤ Conducted audits.

➤ Supervised 5 staff auditors on statewide basis.

Internal Revenue Service, Reno District   1981-1982

Internal Revenue Agent—Field Audit

➤ Conducted audits of individuals, partnerships and corporations as to
Federal income taxes.

Nevada State Treasury, Division of Taxation   1980-1981
Auditor-Accountant: Field

➤ After college graduation, began as auditor-accountant trainee in
corporate tax bureau.
➤ Then assigned as Field Auditor responsible for individual audits of
corporations as to state taxes.

CERTIFICATIONS AND COMMENDATIONS

Certified Police Instructor

Since 1987, Division Lecturer on various types of
White-Collar Crime, Organized Crime and Official Corruption.

Specialized presentations on:

- Arson for Profit,
- Money Laundering, and
- Counterfeiting.

Certificate of Commendation
Upperville County Prosecutor's Office

Letter of Commendation
United States Congressman Martin Shulman

Letter of Commendation
Donald O'Connor
1st Assistant Attorney General and Director of Criminal Justice

Letter of Commendation
Dr. Saul Valvanis, Commissioner
Nevada Department of Education

Letter of Commendation
Commissioner Mary Purcello
Nevada Department of Banking

Letters of Commendation from
Various Societies and Organizations

American Bankers Association
Northern and Southern Districts of Nevada

American Society for Industrial Security Officers

Petroleum Security Officers Association

Nevada State University
Accounting Society

Nevada Commission of Investigation (S.C.I.)

Others as to state employment

Citation: Nevada State Assembly
as to community work with Scouts as Cubmaster

1999-present
Certified Public Manager Program
Continuing program sponsored by
Nevada Department of Personnel and Reno University.

1999
Roundtable: Money Laundering
Two-day seminar held at Main Treasury Building, Washington, D.C.,
sponsored by U.S. Assistant Secretary of Treasury.

1997
Supervising Undercover Investigations
Four-day course sponsored by the **University of Delaware** concentrating on covert
narcotics and organized-crime investigations.

1992
Racketeer Influenced Corrupt Organization (R.I.C.O.)
Sponsored by Nevada Division of Criminal Justice. 1 week course.
Also participated as Instructor for "Interpreting Financial Statements."

1991
Seminar: White Collar Crime-Investigation and Prosecution
1 week. Battelle Institute, Seattle, Washington
Also participated as Instructor as to utilizing the "Net Worth" approach
as an investigative technique.

1985
Special Agent Training: Intelligence Division, U.S. Treasury
As State Investigator, completed 8-week course at National Training Center
in Washington, D.C., by enrollment in class of Federal Agents. Final two weeks was
Inter-Agency training with Secret Service, Securities & Exchange Commission, F.B.I.,
and Bureau of Alcohol, Tobacco & Firearms.

Firearms Training and Personal Defense
Police Academy, Upperville County - 2 weeks.

Investigation of White-Collar Crime and Official Corruption
Sponsored by **Seton Hall University** in conjunction with
Peat, Marwick & Mitchell. 2-week course.

1984
Advanced Training for State Auditors
Held at Federal Inter-Agency Training Center, San Diego, CA. 3 weeks.

1982
Basic Training for State Auditors
Held at the Federal Inter-Agency Training Center, San Diego, CA. 3 weeks.

1981
Internal Revenue Agent Training
Held in Philadelphia, PA. This 7-week course included education and
application of Taxation Code, Regs, Cases and Rulings, and audit procedures.

SPECIALIZED TRAINING AND COURSES. contd.

On other various dates received specialized training held at
Division of Criminal Justice such as related to:

- Wiretap and Electronic Surveillance,
- Grand Jury Training,
- Search and Seizure, etc.

EDUCATION

1980   B.S., Commerce, Reno College
         Major: Business Administration/Accounting

         Post-degree coursework in:
         Taxation, Investments, and Computers

1987   Passed Nevada State examination for Investment Securities
         Brokers and Dealers
         Received principal rating.

current Certified Public Manager program,
         in conjunction with Nevada State University
         Completed two of three sessions.

OUTSIDE ACTIVITIES

Cubmaster - Pack 60
Cub Scouts, Cash-in-Hand, Nevada

Trustee and Treasurer
Robert Jordan Memorial Scholarship Fund

PERSONAL

Married, 3 children
Age - 43
Height - 6'3"
Weight - 218 lbs.

Sara: Overcoming Her Background

Sara had spent some time as an actor. When corporate hiring managers saw this on the résumé, they didn't want to see her. It overshadowed the solid corporate experience she already had. What's more, if she did get in for an interview, managers probed to find out why she had chosen acting as a career. It made her business experience look less substantial.

On her revised résumé, of which we have included only the first page, a summary statement puts a corporate spin on her theater experience (which included more than acting) and highlights her education more.

In addition, she dropped the name of the second company on her résumé (Golden Bo Tree East Co.), since it is irrelevant and distracting.

When testing your résumé in the market, notice if anything about your background is operating as a handicap for you. Think of how you can reposition this part to downplay it and how you can highlight those parts you want the reader to focus on.

SARA G. HARRIS

355 South York Avenue
New York, New York 10483

Home: (212) 555-2351
Office: (212) 555-3320

EXPERIENCE

Amrock, New York
1996 - Present

Management Development Associate. In-house Corporate Human Resources consultant. Developed, designed and implemented vehicles to enhance Human Resource professionalism within Amrock world-wide. Accomplishments include:

- Executive Development - Created and implemented nomination process whereby top performers are selected to attend Executive Education programs. Coordinated the entire process, serving as a liaison between the university and participants to ensure appropriate developmental match.

- High Potential Development - Initiated database to: identify and source candidates for potential job assignments, track institutional progress and follow up on development plans.

- Focus Groups - Assessment of Development Needs - Managed all aspects of project design and implementation: met with senior management, prepared protocol, conducted sessions with over 120 HR professionals both in the U.S. and Europe, and analyzed and integrated data.

- Questionnaire Development - Designed feedback instrument for HR professionals worldwide to elicit recommendations on key HR development needs.

- Program Development - Researched and designed seminars for senior human resources offsite. Included compensation seminars on Incentive Plan Design, Long Term Incentive and Tax Effective Comp. Coached presenters through feedback sessions.

Golden Bo Tree East Co., Ltd., Bangkok,Thailand
1995

Organization Development Consultant. Process consultant to senior management on cross-cultural issues around goal clarification, decision making, and team building. Resulted in improved organizational effectiveness in adapting to Thailand business demands.

Actor
1987 - 1993

EDUCATION

Columbia University, New York, New York; **Master of Arts**-Organizational Psychology   1995 - 1996
Awarded Academic Scholarship-3.7 G.P.A.

New York University, New York, New York; **Master of Arts**-Counseling Psychology   1993 - 1995
Awarded Academic Scholarship-3.6 G.P.A.

Utah State University, Bachelor of Fine Arts-Acting   1983 - 1987
     Awarded Full Tuition Scholarship

PUBLICATIONS

A Case Study: Organization Development in a Health Care System
New York University Psychology Quarterly - September, 1995

ADDITIONAL INFORMATION

Languages: Thai
Affiliations: American Psychological Association; NY Organization Development Network
Computer Skills: Mac OS, Software - Microsoft Office '98; SPSSX

SARA G. HARRIS

355 South York Avenue
New York, New York 10483

Home: (212) 555-2351
Office: (212) 555-3320

Management/Organization Development Specialist

**Over 8 years of development and stand-up experience.
Financial, Entertainment and Exporting Industries.**

- Proven consulting expertise in:

- Executive and High Potential Development
- Needs Assessment
- Organizational Research

- Two masters' degrees in Organizational and Counseling Psychology.

- Extensive exposure in Southeast Asia; fluent in Thai.

Professional Experience

Amrock, New York   1994 - Present

Manager of Management Development

In-house Corporate Human Resources consultant. Developed, designed and implemented vehicles to enhance the professionalism of over 2,000 officers worldwide.

Accomplishments include:

- **High-Potential Development**
  Assess and identify top performers to: meet specific business talent needs, attend Executive University programs, and facilitate succession planning.

- **Executive Development**
  Created and implemented nomination process whereby top performers are selected to attend executive education programs. Coordinated the entire process, serving as a liaison between the university and participants to ensure appropriate developmental match.

- **Focus Groups - Assessment of Development Needs**
  Managed all aspects of project design and implementation: met with senior management, prepared protocol, conducted sessions with over 500 officers throughout the U.S. and Europe, and analyzed and integrated data.

- **Organizational Research**
  Use of statistical and research design (SPSSX) to conduct surveys, climate studies, turnover studies. Designed feedback instrument for HR professionals worldwide to elicit recommendations on key training needs.

- **Program Development**
  Researched and designed seminars for senior offsite. Included compensation seminars on Incentive Plan Design, Long Term Incentive and Tax Effective Compensation. Coached presenters through feedback sessions.

Richard: Functional Résumé Within Chronological

Richard had worked in essentially the same job for well over twenty years. Having opted for early retirement, he considered going in two completely different directions. One was a continuation of his present career in private banking—a field that was very tight. His second option was a lot more fun: he could see himself in an administrative role—for a major foundation or art museum, or even working for a decorating firm.

Richard had strong administrative skills, and a wealth of experience in activities outside of his regular job. He served as the treasurer of a not-for-profit organization, and he also served for many years as the president of his cooperative apartment building.

One résumé emphasizes his banking background; the other presents a more rounded person and gives more weight to his extracurricular experiences.

The banking résumé is also an example of functional information presented within a chronological format.

M. RICHARD KUNSTLER

71 South 44th Street
New York, NY 10001

Home: (212) 555-1111
Office: (212) 559-0000

SUMMARY OF QUALIFICATIONS

An administrative manager with broad experience in running operations. In-depth work with accountants, lawyers, agents, and so on. Over 20 years' experience as a trust officer handling all aspects of fiduciary relationships for PremierBank's private banking clients (175 families with overall networth of $400 million). Expert in all financial arrangements (trust and estate accounts, asset management, non-profit, and tenant shareholder negotiations), as well as real estate matters. Have worked with New York's most prestigious law firms. Extensive experience in staffing.

PROFESSIONAL EXPERIENCE

PREMIERBANK - PRIVATE BANKING DIVISION   **1975 - PRESENT**

<u>Relationship Manager</u>

Responsible for overall management of 175 family relationships having an over-all net worth of $400 million. Coordinated trust, investment advisory, custodial and banking services. Coordinate co-trustees, attorneys, accountants and beneficiaries.

o Saved family $3 million in taxes up front by the use of an innovative estate-planning method.

o Developed a complete estate plan for a family whose financial arrangements were in disarray: they had archaic wills and no tax planning in the event of death. Resulted in their having appropriate wills, trusts for children, investment account for wife with gifted securities and a new attorney and accountant.

o Broad knowledge of discretionary powers, fiduciary accounting, tax applications and investment requirements.

o Reviewed complex financial situations, weighing options vis-a-vis income payments, gifts and estate impact. As liaison between family members, attorney and advisors, formulated annual financial programs saving one client $30,000 annually in taxes.

o As consultant to a wealthy family in jeopardy of losing $600-million income flow and having U.S. assets attached, analyzed all accounts determining precise options available. Evolved a plan through the use of assignments and off-shore corporations to preserve income and assets.

President, 71 SOUTH 44TH STREET CORPORATION INC.   1989 - Present

o **Run a premiere building - set very high standards.**

o Closely direct the managing agent and superintendent who oversee a staff of 7 serving a 38-unit apartment building. Resulted in minimum turnover of staff and priority attention from the managing agent.

o Screen all prospective tenant shareholder applicants as to financial and personal qualifications. Instituted a new way of dealing with applicants that avoided lawsuits while maintaining apartment quality.

o As President, interface with board of directors on matters of policy, building maintenance, operating expenses and revenues. With Treasurer, chart anticipated capital improvements and budget appropriately.

o Act as liaison with outside counsel.

o Recommended and implemented an innovative revenue concept resulting in greater financial security for the corporation.

Treasurer, THE LOGOS SOCIETY OF NEW YORK   1987 - Present

o **Very much improved the solvency of this organization.**

o Manage operating budget, and track sources of all revenue and expenditures, both operating and capital improvements.

o Coordinate in-house and outside accountants. Monitor all legal and financial matters concerning gifts, legacies, and other actions affecting the organization including contracts.

o Oversee all investments and real estate matters. Sold old headquarters, and recommended the sale of abutting property resulting in financial solvency.

o Monitor staffing requirements. Put in retired businessman to better run the clinic and allow doctors to serve clients.

o Individual fundraising resulted in two $100,000-plus legacies.

o Work with lawyers regarding publishing contracts, leases and other matters.

EDUCATION

New York University	Graduate Courses: Business Law Accounting, Corporate Management	1977
St. Crispin University	B.A., Business Admin./Economics	1974

M. RICHARD KUNSTLER

71 South 44th Street   Office: (212) 559-0000
New York, NY 10001   Office: (212) 555-1111

SUMMARY OF EXPERIENCE

Over 20 years' experience handling all aspects of fiduciary relationships for
**PremierBank's private clients: (175 families with overall net worth of $400 mil-
lion).** Successfully increased revenue through new business efforts, client cultivation and account assessment. Consistently achieved fee increases resulting
in bonus awards. Work well with high-net-worth individuals.

PROFESSIONAL EXPERIENCE

PREMIERBANK - PRIVATE BANKING DIVISION   **1975 - PRESENT**

RELATIONSHIP MANAGER - Private Banking Division   1987 - Present
TRUST OFFICER - Investment Management Group   1980 - 1987

Handle all aspects of fiduciary relationships for PremierBank's private banking
clients: 175 families with overall net worth of $400 million.

o   As a seasoned account officer, assigned the most difficult, time-consuming
    accounts that presumably had the lowest potential. Turned the accounts
    around. Achieved fee increases. Received bonuses.

o   Recently gained an $18-million will appointment one week before person's
    death. Generated $350,000 fee.

o   Saved family $3 million in taxes up front by the use of an innovative estate
    planning method.

o   Developed a complete estate plan for a family whose financial arrangements
    were in disarray: they had archaic wills and no tax planning in the event
    of death. Resulted in their having appropriate wills, trusts for children,
    investment account for wife with gifted securities and a new attorney and
    accountant.

AREAS OF SPECIAL COMPETENCE

Client Relations

o   Identified 50 cases (20% of account base) where client dissatisfaction
    existed. Established one-on-one contact to identify problem areas. Insti-
    tuted aggressive service campaigns and quarterly review meetings. Within
    two years gained confidence of 96% of dissatisfied customers. Obtained
    $26 million in new business and retained a vulnerable $10-million account.

o   Recognized importance of interfacing with several hundred attorneys, ac-
    countants and financial advisors. Maintained high profile through constant
    contact and briefings. Won their esteem. Resulted in a greater working
    compatibility, efficient decision-making and gaining new business. In one
    instance, obtained a $60-million account relationship.

Consulting

o Reviewed complex financial situations, weighing options vis-a-vis income payments, gifts and estate impact. As liaison between family members, attorney and advisors, formulated annual financial programs saving one client $30 million annually in taxes.

o In capacity as a consultant to a wealthy family in jeopardy of losing $600-million income flow and having U.S. assets attached, analyzed all accounts determining precise options available. Evolved a plan through the use of assignments and off-shore corporations to preserve income and assets.

Analysis and Planning

o Evaluated requests for special payments of capital assets and income. Assessed propriety of payments, researching provisions covering such discretionary actions, consulting with attorneys, family members and accountants. Processed and documented approximately 75 requests annually with 100% of recommendations being accepted.

o Developed improved alternatives to outdated operational procedures. Formulated a new plan for handling over 1,500 telephone requests during a 2-month period. Coordinated with operation department to establish direct customer wire into central information center eliminating 5,000 unnecessary calls. In another instance, developed Form Letters reducing expense in responding by 95%.

o Analyzed 260 accounts for substandard fees. Developed a strategic plan to align revenue with services. Aggressive action and persistence resulted in fee increases adding $200 million to revenues annually.

EDUCATION

New York University	Graduate Courses: Business Law, Accounting, Corporate Management	1977
St. Crispin University	BA, Business Admin./Economics	1974

ASSOCIATIONS

Director of cooperative apartment building   1988 - Present
    President of Board in 1989. Operating budget $650 million.

Director of The Logos Society of New York   1987 - Present
    Served as Vice President. Treasurer in 1988.
    Operating budget $1 million.

Philippe: Aiming for Very Different Targets

When a man is in turmoil how shall he find peace
Save by staying patient till the stream clears?
How can a man's life keep its course
If he will not let it flow?
Those who flow as life flows know
They need no other force:
They feel no wear, They feel no tear,
They need no mending, no repair.
Lao Tzu, *Tao de Ching*
Translated by Witter Bynner

We do not succeed in changing things according to
our desire, but gradually our desire changes.
The situation that we hoped to change because it was
intolerable becomes unimportant. We have not man-
aged to surmount the obstacle, as we were absolutely
determined to do, but life has taken us round it,
led us past it, and then if we turn round to gaze at the
remote past, we can barely catch sight of it,
so imperceptible has it become.
Marcel Proust

I'm very lucky. If it wasn't for golf, I don't know what
I'd be doing. If my IQ had been two points lower,
I'd have been a plant somewhere.
Lee Travino, as quoted in *Golfweek*

S ince he was looking for a job anyway, Philippe thought he might as well explore two targets: one in his current field (purchasing); and one having to do with his passion (sports).

He would need two résumés, since these were such different targets. Many job hunters think they need different résumés for every target they are going after. But usually the fields that interest you are not as different as they may seem. For instance, Norman Neumann, whose résumé we saw earlier, had wanted one for the fashion industry and one for a job search outside that industry. In fact, one résumé served both purposes.

Philippe ended up with an excellent position in the purchasing field—one very close to home, and with an increase in salary.

But his exploration of the sports field helped him understand just how important it was in his life. As it happens, managing cycling events was central to his family life. His entire family participated in running an annual event, and he was unwilling to give it up. After Philippe negotiated the salary for the new job, he told the hiring manager that he had been an Olympic cyclist and that he was committed to running the annual cycling event in his town, a project that took two weeks of his and his family's time. Philippe asked if "there was any way" he could get an extra two weeks off every year to run the event.

The company agreed to the extra time off—with pay—and offered to sponsor the event!

Philippe Mardig

47 Courbet Plaza
Bernini Square, MS 55700

Home: (555) 555-7844
Business: (222) 555-5564

Innovative Purchasing Department Head ($55 million annually) with a high level of integrity and over 15 years at Amdahl. Experience in automation, equipment evaluation, forms management and data processing. Created a divisional Purchasing Department resulting in $4-million savings. Served as Corporate Fleet Administrator (a fleet of 1,300) and Contracts Negotiator resulting in savings of $2.4 million.

EXPERIENCE

AMDAHL   1982 - Present

PURCHASING MANAGER   1997 - Present
Amdahl Properties

Supervise staff of 8 in Purchasing and 6 in Payables, $55-million annual volume, 3,600 purchase orders processed annually.

- Selected to <u>**create divisional purchasing department**</u> where none previously existed.

  - <u>**Served as the standard for other Amdahl purchasing departments**</u>.
  - Trained managers to set up other purchasing departments.
  - A professionally-run model operation set up as a profit center, charging for our services.
  - Set up automated purchasing system.
  - Produced a total package of controls to inform management regarding spending.
  - Developed an MIS interface with fixed asset, financial control, and the corporate technology areas.
  - Consistently exceeded goals set by minority/women's vendor program.

- Consistently developed innovative cost-saving methods.

  - <u>**Saved $4 million**</u> through creation of computer and copier lease analysis program.
  - Renegotiated corporate discount on personal computers from 15% to 35%, resulting in <u>**savings of $1 million**</u>.
  - Created a surplus and trade-in program resulting in a <u>**savings of $200,000**</u>.

- Wrote the *Purchasing Policy Manual*

  - Served as a prototype for other divisions in Amdahl.
  - Evaluated personal computers, desktop publishing, facsimile, microfilm, office and other equipment.

- Preparation of all budget and financial reports.

- <u>Published purchasing newsletter</u> for distribution to other purchasing departments, financial controllers, and endusers.

SENIOR BUYER   1995 - 1997
AMDAHL Corporate Purchasing Department

- Rated #1 buyer.
- Assisted in the purchase of $50 million annually of computers and related equipment.
- Negotiated national and short-term contracts for corporate and specific needs.
- Served as Corporate Fleet Administrator
    - Fleet of 1,330 vehicles.
    - **Saved $2.4 million** through renegotiation of lease.
    - Supervised fleet administrators throughout United States.
    - Developed recommended vehicle list with emphasis on reduced operating costs.
    - Set up mailroom operation for AMDAHL Delaware.

CITIBANK Corporate Payables Department   1992 - 1994
Senior Operator/Assistant Systems Analyst

- Involved in selection, testing and installation of new equipment.
- Project coordinator for implementation of online purchasing system.
- Served as telecommunications intermediary for in-house and external clients.
- Handled leasing requirements of users.

CITIBANK Corporate Machine Repair   1985 - 1991
Senior Service Technician

- Service full range of microfilm equipment and automated filing systems.
- Supervise equipment warehouse facility for storage and distribution of surplus.
- Renegotiated replacement parts purchase discount resulting in a savings of $300,000.

SPERRY RAND CORPORATION   1980 - 1985

Territorial responsibility for service of complete line of microfilm and automated filing systems.

EDUCATION

A.A.S., Business   City University of New York

Philippe Mardig

47 Courbet Plaza
Bernini Square, MS 55700

Home: (555) 555-7844
Business: (222) 555-5564

SUMMARY OF QUALIFICATIONS

A lifetime involvement in competitive sports – participation, administration and promotion. Ongoing relationships with corporate sponsors and local governments. Personal connections with TV, radio and newspapers to bring events to the public. Work closely with The U.S. Cycling Federation. Manage cycling championships. Won over 100 races including 3rd place <u>1988 Olympic Trials</u>. Former <u>President of MSSC</u>. <u>Annually promote the largest race in the state</u>. Persuasive detail-oriented manager who overcomes obstacles to successfully complete projects.

PARTICIPATION

Extensive athletic background including scholastic involvement in gymnastics, track and karate, and amateur-level weight lifting and cycling.

- National Cycling Champion, 1972
- 3rd Place 1972 Olympic Trials - kilometer
- Won over 100 races.

ASSOCIATION POSITIONS HELD

Utilized expertise and personal contacts to successfully organize, develop and present cycling events exhibitions to showcase cycling to business, and potential sponsoring organizations.
<u>President, GBSC</u>

- Secured sponsorship of Windsor bicycles.
- Put together a national-level team including 6 state, national and Olympic winners.
- Oversaw or directed:
  - awards banquet,
  - annual racing program and
  - 5 races.
- Served as media contact.

<u>President and Founder</u>, Missouri Bicycle Club

Formed to promote development of Olympic cyclists in the state.
- Organized the 7-Eleven Missouri Cycling Classics.
  - Worked with sponsors, government, Chamber of Commerce.
  - Directed it for 5 years.
- Brought Olympic-level cycling (featuring Eric Heyden) to Missouri.
- Served as media contact.

<u>Race Chairman</u>, Missouri Wheelman

- Conducted weight lifting and training clinics.
- Directed the Missouri County Cycling Classic.
- Secured sponsorship from bicycle companies.
- Served as media contact.

GOVERNMENT-RELATED EVENTS RUN

Successfully work with governments and government agencies to secure necessary service (police and ambulance), highway sanitation. Coordinate mailings and promotions with government PR people, sports units, Chambers of Commerce. Examples include:

- U.S.C.F.
  - Meet regularly with The District Representative.
  - Meet weekly with The Assistant Executive Director to organize National championships.
  - Arrange housing, food and welcoming reception.

- Eliot County, Department of Recreation and Parks
  - Handle every detail. Close contact covering every detail from sign making and banners to securing showmobile platform, hiring the announcer and phototimer.
  - Coordinate publicity and distribute information with Sports Unit.
  - Work with Commissioner to handle logistics.
  - Work with Sponsorship Coordinator to attract sponsors.
  - Missouri Tourism Bureau

- For major events, secure the cooperation of all the governments and agencies involved.

PROMOTE MAJOR EVENTS

- Served as cycling spokesperson for Missouri.
- 7-Eleven Cycling Classic
  - Initiated and developed this national event.
  - Recruited Eric Heyden and other members of the Olympic Team.
  - Handled all details for 5 years.
  - Served as the media contact.
  - Secured the sponsorship of 7-Eleven.
- Put together programs for events (coordinate typesetters, printers, etc.)
- Interface with all major media: radio, TV and print. Personally know all the reporters and editors.
- Outstanding Citizen Award from Eliot County, 1999.

Other Events Promoted:

Missouri Cycling Classic	Giacometti Dave Cycling Classic
Eliot Country Cycling Classic	1997 Masters National Criterion Championships
Byron Lake	Halloween Cycling Classic

SECURED CORPORATE SPONSORS

7-Eleven	Hewlett-Packard	Nynex
Manchester	Epson	NEC
	Saven	

ALSO HAVE EXTENSIVE CORPORATE EXPERIENCE

The Five O'Clock Club®

George: Positioned for a New Field After "Retirement"

The earth is a place to live in, where we must put up
with sights, with sounds, with smells, too, by Jove!—
breathe dead hippo, so to speak, and not be
contaminated. And there, don't you see? Your
strength comes in, the faith in your ability for the
digging of unostentatious holes to bury the stuff in—
your power of devotion, not to yourself,
but to an obscure, backbreaking business.
Joseph Conrad, *Heart of Darkness*

George had spent his career life on Wall Street. At the young age of fifty, he decided to take early retirement. He knew he could easily work for another twenty years and felt that it was better to make his move now rather than wait until he was older. Luckily, George already knew that he wanted to teach in a private high school. (If *you* are not clear about what you could do next, start with our book *Targeting the Job You Want*.)

George made one slight error: given his excellent background, he thought that the not-for-profit world would jump at the chance to hire him. After all, he had been a successful executive and had worked in academia earlier in his career. But being accomplished is not enough. Every industry wants people who *fit in* well: people don't want their organization disrupted by outsiders. The world of Wall Street (competitive, brusque) is very different from the world of academia (collegial, slower-paced). After a few meetings, George realized he was going to have problems getting in—unless he changed.

George needed to look, act and dress the part for his new role: a less starchy appearance, a slightly longer haircut than he was used to (though still well-groomed), and a lot less aggressive in his speech and manner. Wall Street had left its mark on George, and his current persona would likely be off-putting in academia.

Rather than rush out and meet more people in academia right away, George needed to settle into a new mindset. His demeanor slowly changed as he developed his list of schools to contact and then sent for and studied school bulletins. George became more relaxed, started to speak more slowly, and actually started to look more appropriate for the industry he had targeted. There had been another George hidden under the Wall Street veneer.

Now he needed an appropriate résumé. When making a career change, the strategy is to put at the top of your résumé the things that would be of most interest to your target market. Because George had been sincerely interested in education for quite some time, even when he was on Wall Street, he had taken on a few education-related assignments. For example, he had recruited graduates from major universities to work at his Wall Street firm.

George highlighted those experiences and his earlier experiences in education at the top of his résumé. In the body of his résumé, he went into some depth about his most recent position, which was impressive. However, the bulk of his résumé highlighted only the experiences that he thought would be of interest to those in academia. He simply listed with no supporting detail those jobs that would be of no interest to those in academia.

Now, rather than thinking he would just walk into a job in academia, George humbled himself a little and asked for meetings to gather information about how he could get in. He was very well received and was given a lot of good advice.

Within a few short months, George had landed two part-time assignments at excellent secondary schools. George was paying his dues, learning the system and would soon become settled in his new field. He could see that it was only a matter of time before he would be working the number of hours he wanted in the field he had dreamt about for so long.

GEORGE THOMAS
78 Silver Ridge Road   Stamford, CT 99999   (555) 555-2475

SENIOR EXECUTIVE

• **Program Director**   • **Top Recruiter**   • **Educator**

- Started, organized and managed nontraditional MBA training program; taught for 16 years.
- For 10 years, headed recruiting at major universities: University of Chicago, University of Pennsylvania (Wharton School), University of Virginia (Darden), Dartmouth University (Amos Tuck).
    - Recruited at both the MBA and BA levels.
- Ran Citibank's highest profile college recruiting program.
- Managing Director/Trading Manager, Citibank Securities, Inc.
    - $30 billion under management, amounting to 10% of the bank's assets.
    - Revenue of over $160 million in 11 years.
- Private school educator and department head.
- PhD candidate (ABD), MA, BA, The Catholic University of America.
- Edited series of 15 books, *The European Religious Experience.*

A leader with substantial hands-on experience.
An individual whose personal philosophy and values
have enabled him to succeed and to inspire and lead others.

CITIBANK SECURITIES, INC. — 1980- Present

Managing Director; Trading Manager (1985 - Present)

As a senior officer, started, organized and managed a highly profitable business.
- Built a highly visible business responsible for financing the bank's U.S. Treasury positions.
- Achieved $30 billion under management, which amounted to 10% of Citibank's balance sheet.
- Managed a team of 6 senior traders.
- Earned revenue over $160 million in 11 years.
- Managed significant profit and loss with senior risk authority.
- Oversaw all compliance, legal, systems and operational issues

Citibank MBA Program (1982 - Present)
In keeping with corporate philosophy that line managers should be actively involved in recruiting and training: started, organized and managed the first nontraditional MBA training program at Citibank.

Training:
- Developed new programs involving 20-30 line managers as trainers.
- Built on MBA classroom knowledge with presentations of a practical nature.
- The three-month program trained 50 individuals from top universities.
- Personally taught in the program for 16 years, including technical modules on the financing businesses, selling skills and the government securities markets. Also presented a special series on elements of a successful career in the financial services industry.

Recruiting:
- For 10 years a leading recruiter at major universities, including University of Chicago, University of Pennsylvania (Wharton), University of Virginia (Darden) and Dartmouth (Amos Tuck).
- Recruited at both the MBA and BA levels.
- Extensive on-campus and in-house interviewing experience. Presented to groups of 40 to 300.
- Served as relationship manager for the Amos Tuck School at Dartmouth University.

Manager, College Recruiting (1984)

- Hired 50 people from top 10 universities.
- Organized and delivered presentations, managed MBA recruiting schedules, follow-up and closure process for all candidates.
- For the first time, involved senior management in the recruiting process by inviting prospects to the firm.

Vice President and Assistant Sales Manager, Government Bond Department (1983)
Sales Person, Government Bond Department (1980)

GOLDMAN SACHS AND CO., New York, NY   1979 - 1980
Sales Person. Responsible for individual Accounts in Commodities Division.

DATONA BROTHERS, INC., San Juan, Puerto Rico   1975 - 1979
Vice President of family-owned wholesale hardware firm.
- As member of management team introduced 5 new product lines into local market.
- Succeeded in becoming fluent in Spanish, while mastering Latin business culture.

SCHOOL OF THE HOLY CROSS, Potomac, MD   1973 - 1975
Head of Religion Department
- Developed curriculum, taught upper-level courses in Western Religious Thought and Greek.

ST. LUKE SCHOOL, Robertson, MD   1966 - 1973
- Developed, managed and taught in the Parish Adult Education program, which resulted in expanded educational opportunities for entire neighborhood.

EDUCATION

THE CATHOLIC UNIVERSITY OF AMERICA, Washington, DC

PhD Candidate (ABD), Department of Religious Studies, 1975
Area of Concentration: Philosophical Theology

MA, Department of Religious Studies, 1973; Minor, Philosophy

BA, Department of Religious Studies, 1971; Minor, Anthropology

ARTICLES

"Dialectical Panentheism: Rahner and Hegel"
The Irish Theological Quarterly, Vol. XLII, No. 2, April 1975

PERSONAL

Married, Three children	Member, CAEL and The Alliance
Fluent in Spanish	Interests: American History, The Civil War
Reading knowledge in French and German	Classical Music, Poetry
Securities Registrations, Series 7, 63, 24	Boy Scouts of America, Council Member
Special Olympics, Spring 1998	Troop 70, New Canaan, CT, 1987-1994

Various Résumés for Managers and Professionals

They can have anything they want, but they can't have everything they want. There is more to life than Kansas. The key is choosing what we want most (our heart's desire), letting go of everything else we want (for now), and moving (mentally, emotionally and physically) toward our goal.

John-Roger and Peter McWilliams,
Do It! Let's Get Off Our Buts

". . . sir, I would like to become a psychologist, but it requires so much training that I'm afraid I would be too old when I finish."

The wise man sat in silence for a few moments, smiled, and then asked, "Young lady, how long would it take you to become a psychologist?"

"About seven years," she replied.

"How old would you be then?" was the next question.

"I will be twenty-five."

Then the man asked, "How old will you be in seven years if you don't become a psychologist?"

Of course, her answer was the same. "Well, I guess I would be about twenty-five."

Time waits for no one. . . Remember, your future is exactly what you make it.

Dennis Kimbro,
Think and Grow Rich: A Black Choice

On the following pages are additional résumés for people of various levels. In each case, the person thought about his or her target area, and positioned his or her background to fit the target.

Now, take a crack at your own résumé. Then test it with friends. Ask them, "When you look at this résumé, how do I come across?"

That's a very specific question, and you're looking for a very specific answer.

The danger here is that, when you ask people for comments, you may get a host of suggestions about things *that don't matter*. Don't get derailed, for example, by amateurish advice about résumé length. Pay attention to criticisms that have to do with the way you are *positioned*. If you intend to come across as someone who manages people, but the reader sees you as a person who has written press releases, that's a problem worth paying attention to. If your friends don't get the point, chances are hiring managers won't either. Some people think they're being helpful by suggesting word or punctuation changes: some of these may be different but not necessarily better.

Incorporate all valuable suggestions, of course, but use friends and associates to help fine tune the *positioning of the résumé*—then hit your target areas.

Archibald Alexander
25 Campanas Street
Santa Fe, NM 87555
505-555-6281

<u>SUMMARY OF QUALIFICATIONS</u>

14 years experience in design and administration in **all areas of employee benefit plans**, including 5 years with **Briar Consultants**. Advised some of the largest and most prestigious companies in the country. Excellent training and communications skills. MBA in Finance. **An effective manager who delivers consistent results**.

NYNAX CORPORATION   1993 - Present
Manager, Stock Plans Administration

Manage an 8-person unit administering Employee Stock Purchase and Executive Stock Option plans.

- o   Personal contact with the **4,000 most senior executives**.
- o   Accounting and record keeping for **$178 million** in plan assets.
- o   **Reduced expenses 25%** through automation and productivity enhancements.
- o   Successfully conducted major stock purchase plan offering on tight schedule; the largest the company had ever undertaken: **90 countries**; data from 16 payroll systems; distribution of personalized packages to 60,000 employees.
- o   Implemented state-of-the-art transaction confirmations system.

BANKERS FIRST COMPANY   1992 - 1993
Defined Contribution Plans Manager

Managed unit of six; **$750 million in plan assets**; 25 client plans.

- o   Managed all record keeping, trust and administrative services for very large corporate clients' savings, 401(K) and stock ownership plans.
- o   Handled all regulatory and ERISA compliance, cash and securities management, consulting, trust administration and accounting.
- o   **Reduced overtime 50%; computer usage 25%; expenses 33%**.

BRIAR CONSULTANTS   1987 - 1992
Defined Contributions Plans Consultant

Managed a unit of 10 consulting on **all phases** of design, implementation and administration of Fortune 500 company plans.

- o   **Increased profits 170%**.
- o   Handled 25 accounts worth $3.2 million in annual revenue.
- o   Managed plan, systems and database design.
- o   Supervised system conversions and daily production.
- o   Performed market analysis.
- o   Delivered sales presentations.
- o   Negotiated contracts and fees.
- o   Designed reports, statements and administrative forms.

146   © 1999, The Five O'Clock Club®, Inc.

BRIAR CONSULTANTS, INC. (Cont'd)
Defined Benefit Plans Manager

o Consulted on pension plan design and interpretation, governmental reporting and compliance, record keeping, administrative practices and procedures and the development and use of compliance manuals.
o Introduced standardized administration manuals and paperwork reduction techniques which **generated more than $1.2 million in consulting revenue**.

ROYAL INSURANCE COMPANY   1986 - 1987
Assistant Manager, Employee Benefits

o Compliance Officer.
o Administered the company's pension, health and other employee benefit plans.
o Performed medical plan cost containment study and implemented changes resulting in a leveling of insurance premiums.
o Offered and implemented HMOs.
o Negotiated insurance contracts with carriers.
o Performed statistical compensation analysis.

NATIONAL BULK CARRIERS   1986
Employee Benefits Manager

Administered domestic and overseas pension and group medical, life, disability and worker's compensation insurance plans. **Secretary Pension and Employee Benefits Committees**.

STANDARD BRANDS INCORPORATED (now RJR Nabisco)   1983 - 1986
Assistant Pension Supervisor

Administered 12 domestic pension plans covering 23,000 bargaining and non-bargaining employees.

EDUCATION

MBA, Economics and Finance, June 1990
BA, Psychology, June 1981
ST. JOHN'S UNIVERSITY

Helen Louise Albelo

44 Cliff Lake Town
Clarksville, New York 10001
Business: 914-555-2550
Residence: 914-555-4557

Summary of Qualifications

8 years' executive experience managing facilities and support services.
Managed and developed **9 service departments** with a **staff of 120**. Reorganized and set quality standards to reduce costs and lower turnover. Implemented training programs, improved morale and the respect of workers for each other. Strong negotiation skills. Work with high technology applications. In a building of 50,000 sq. ft., responsible for **office planning, telecommunications, maintenance, record retention** and company promotion.

Professional Experience

VICE PRESIDENT, OPERATIONS & SUPPORT SERVICES   1989-present
THE KELLOGG GROUP (A subsidiary of Time, Inc.)

Manage a **staff of 120** in **9 service departments**.
Responsible for all **facilities management** for a **50,000 sq. ft. office**.
Manage a budget of **$7-10 million**.
Report directly to the Chairman.

Budgeting, Management and Cost Control
- Manage internal costs. Regularly renegotiate and monitor contracts to **keep costs down**.
- Conduct special analyses and cost comparisons, and purchase research.
- Regularly develop innovative solutions that cut costs in both the short- and long-term.
- Control work overflow resulting in a **smooth-running operation** with few complaints.
- Set up **system to handle bottlenecks and crisis deadlines**.

Telephones
- Select and maintain a system of **300 phones**: **central to this telemarketing business.**
- Establish special relationships with MCI, WATS, FAX , TELEX.
  - Allows for **special testing**, such as the 96 local lines that were installed for a 3-week test period and removed.
- Developed **a system that never goes down**.

Construction and Maintenance
- Regularly manage demolition and construction of space ranging from 3,000 to 7,000 sq. ft.
- Handle all city filings, HVAC regulations and fire alarm systems.
- Handle all design and decoration including carpets, furniture, lighting and wall coverings.
- Maintain 50,000 sq. ft.: floors, walls and so on.
- Negotiate/maintain cleaning contracts and maintenance contracts for business machines.

Records Retention
Manage the storage of **30,000 sq. ft. of records.**
- Established a successful **system for quick recall and timely destruction.**
- **Cut storage costs by two-thirds.**

<u>VICE PRESIDENT, OPERATIONS & SUPPORT SERVICES</u>, contd.

<u>Printing and Mailings</u>
- Coordinate writing, approval process, and actual printing:
  - company brochures,
  - redesign of company logo and
  - annual Christmas card (designed by kids at Ronald McDonald House).
- Maintain company mailing list. Produce mailings, brochures and self-promotional materials.
- Monitor <u>high volume, complex, on-deadline outside printing</u>.

<u>Research Production Department</u>
- <u>Handle 56 million copies/year.</u>
- Set up staff to monitor work flow and productivity of research projects as they pass through various areas of the company.
- Monitor project from proposal letter, questionnaire development, word processing, production, distribution and return, validation checking, coding, keypunching, data processing and final report.

<u>Data Processing</u>
- Staff of 10.
- Develop programs for customized research studies.
- UNIX system.
- Maintain 13 remote PCs that are tied in to the UNIX.

<u>N.Y. State Society of CPS's</u>   1987-1989
Office Manager

- Staff of 10.
- Supervised equipment and production requirements to ensure progressive departmental growth.
- Supported three organizational divisions.

<u>NU Financial Aid Department</u>   1982-1987
Assistant to Loan Officer

<u>Advanced Education</u>

Various technical and managerial courses.

Dr. Carol Jackson

1336 Union Street
Miami, FL 99213
999-555-5803

Summary of Qualifications

20 years' experience in Program Development for universities and agencies.
Managed **projects ranging from $500,000 to $10 million**.
Directed small art museum. **Determined cultural policy for a small country**.
Ed.D. in International Education, University of Massachusetts, Amherst, MA

Areas of Expertise

- **International Education** in developing countries
- **Arts and Museum Administration**
- Securing **grants of $1 to $5 million each**
- Writing, researching and **publishing**
- Teaching English, African and Caribbean Studies, etc.
- Fluent in English and French

Program Development Experience

Institute of Social and Economic Research   1999-2000
University of Trinidad
Research Fellow

- Managed budget of **$1 million** for special project.
- Conducted an analysis of the effects of senior comprehensive schooling on the labor
  market performance of a sample of vocational graduates.
- **Edited 300-page book**.

Director, The National Museum   1997-1999
West Indies

- Designed and managed efforts to secure and maintain **$5 million** in government
  assistance to support museum's efforts.
- **Ran day-to-day operation of the museum**.
- **Trained 50 volunteers**.
- **Arranged exhibitions, lectures, panel discussions**, etc.

Senior Professional   1994-1997
Ministry of Sport, Culture and Youth Affairs, West Indies

- **Wrote national policies** on culture and youth.
- Identified and evaluated socioeconomic trends.
- Advised Minister on strategies for disbursement of **$60-million budget**.

University of Miami Graduate School   1991-1993
and the Puerto Rican Traveling Theater
Coordinator, Performance Education Program for the U.S. Office of Education

- **Administered after-school program** for minority children.
- Annual budget of $500,000 and a client population of 1,000.

University of Michigan   1988-1991
Program Specialist

- Coordinator, The Ghana Project.
- Part of a **$10-million** five-year institutional development project funded by the U.S. Agency for International Development.

Assistant Director   1982-1988
Central Detroit Model Cities
- Administered the Early Childhood Resource Center, catering to inner-city children.

Teaching Experience

Adjunct Lecturer, Ann Arbor College; Africana and Puerto Rican Studies Dept.   1984-1987
Educational Opportunity Center, Detroit; English, GED program   1986-1988
Adjunct Lecturer
    University of Michigan, School of Education   1988-1991
    College of Boca Raton, School of New Resources   1992-1994
    University of the West Indies, Department of Language and Linguistics   1995-2000

Consultancies

Dept. of Indian and Eskimo Affairs, Gov't of Canada
Caribbean/American Community Services Council Inc., N.Y.C.
Oxum International, Miami, Florida
Creative Arts Center, University of the West Indies
Organization of American States, Washington, D.C.
U.S. Agency for International Development/Caricom Secretariat

Professional Affiliations

Phi Delta Kappa
Comparative and International Education Society
Caribbean Studies Association
Anti-Apartheid Organisation of Trinidad and Tobago

Publications

- Carol Jackson (1996, **300 pp.**)
The Independence Experience of The West Indies,
I.S.E.R., Trinidad & Tobago

- **The Vision of Black Artists**;
Carol Jackson (1995)
The Center for African American Art

In Progress:
- Caribbean Contemporary Art
- Focus on Southern Africa

Wilma Albrecht

806 Riverside Estates Road
Altus, N.C. 99712
999-555-9873

Summary of Qualifications

Ten years' freelance experience in writing, editing and proofreading.
Have **edited the writing of at least 45 people.** Backed by 4 years' experience teaching English. Keep balance between respect for the writer's art and the standards set by the organization. Accomplish tasks/goals in an organized, efficient manner with an attitude of pride, sensitivity and self-discipline. Adhere to stylistic standards. B.A. in English.

Professional Experience

Mail Order Manager, Still Pond, Inc.   Jan.-Nov., 1999
Received/processed orders; set up/maintained filing system; corresponded with customers.

Internationally Recognized Not-for-Profit Organization   1984 to 1997
Organization focuses on improving communication techniques, especially in the areas of marriage and family living.

- **Managed a program of 14 presentations a week.**
  - Wrote and delivered 6 different presentations each weekend to groups of 45 people.
  - Edited 8 other presentations each week for 9 years.
  - Critiqued, proofread and **edited the writings of at least 45 other presenters.**
  - Known for thorough, accurate and creative work.
  - Regularly met countless deadlines in both writing and critiquing/editing.

- **Edited bi-monthly newsletter.**
  - Wrote articles for every issue.

- **Co-Director of Operations**, Western North Carolina (1989-1991)
  - Coordinated and gave **final approval of all writing assignments**.
  - Responsible for hiring and firing, budgets and finances.
  - Maintained a balance:
    - sensitivity/respect towards writers and their work,
    - a focus on the final "product" and **meeting standards set by the organizations** and
    - the needs of seminar attendants.
  - **Edited** the organization's **new brochure** (1990).

Altus Elementary School, Parent Volunteer   1984-1993
- Assisted teachers with **proofreading/grading students' creative writing assignments.**
- **Coordinated/edited newspapers** for two class groups.

Teacher, English and Reading   1976-1980
Altus School System, primarily 7th and 8th grades
Focused on grammar/punctuation rules and an appreciation for creative writing and literature.

Education

B.A., English, Altus College, Altus, N.C., 1976
- 3.6 G.P.A. in the 16 English courses taken
- Nominated for Woodrow Wilson Fellowship (1976)
- **Literary Editor** for college yearbook (1975-1976)

PART SEVEN

RÉSUMÉS FOR LOWER-LEVEL PROFESSIONALS

For Junior-Level Employees:
A Summary Makes the Difference

*The greatest discovery of my generation is that
a human being can alter his life by altering
his attitudes of mind.*
William James

---

*Opportunity is missed by most people
because it is dressed in overalls and looks like work.*
Thomas Edison

---

*In the last analysis, the only freedom
is the freedom to discipline ourselves.*
Bernard Baruch

Cecilia is four years out of school; Lillian is a young secretary. In both cases, a summary statement differentiates them from their competitors. Even recent graduates should have a summary—to separate them from all of the other job hunters just out of school.

All résumés—no matter what a person's level is—can include personality traits. It's not enough to know that you have done certain things, it is also relevant to know *how* you did them. Are you especially organized, discreet or innovative? Let the reader know because your personality is one of the most important things you have to offer.

You will notice that the résumés in this book—even that of the most senior executives—mention personality traits. That way readers will get a feeling for the way people accomplish their tasks.

Cecilia Dobbs

499 East Lancaster Avenue
Wayne, PA 19063

(215) 555-1765 (residence)
(215) 555-8024 (office)

Summary of Qualifications

An honors degree in Marketing (<u>magna cum laude</u>) is coupled with <u>four years of professional marketing experience</u> and a solid history of <u>successful projects, promotions and awards</u>. Ability to coordinate the efforts of many to meet organizational goals. High in energy with strong interpersonal skills.

Professional Skills

Hands-on experience within Marketing includes: market research, marketing support, project management, public speaking, training, computers and vendor relations.

Staris Information Services Company

1998 to Present

<u>Marketing Analyst</u>

Supported Product Managers by designing and implementing a variety of projects. Results achieved in this position include:

- Developed contracts, visited branch offices and gave presentations to sales personnel and management.

- Prepared <u>special reports such as the "Analysis of Commercial Revenue"</u> and "Guide to Writing a Proposal."

- Awarded Marketing's "<u>Outstanding Performer</u> of the Month," July, 1999. Received for creatively organizing over 300 pages of material for sales manuals at significant cost savings, ahead of schedule and within one month's time.

- <u>Developed and implemented</u> the <u>contracting system</u> for our division. Made presentations <u>instructing the field</u> on the system's processes. Project in line with goal to reopen channel between marketing and sales force.

- <u>Designed *Product Blue Book*</u>, a handy marketing guide to our products for sales personnel.

- <u>Restructured the *Marketing Guide*</u> to be marketing oriented; previously a marketing policy and procedure manual.

- <u>Created profile questionnaire for a *Competitive Information System*</u>.

- <u>Managed</u> the <u>computerized distribution</u> of several marketing manuals and controlled the content of each.

Bringhan Advertising, Inc.

1997 to 1998

<u>Project Director</u>

Responsible for directing research project of agency clients in the consumer package goods field. Results achieved in this position include:

- <u>Employed various quantitative and qualitative methods</u> for concept tests, taste tests and pre and post-advertising tests.
- Met critical deadline three weeks after hire, one week ahead of schedule.
- Involved in all phases of studies from <u>basic design to client presentation.</u>
- Researched and prepared special report on *Solar Energy Marketplace*.
- Developed strong relations with several research suppliers.

Hilton Research Services   1995 to 1997
Study Director

- Coordinated all production elements for a variety of market research studies including: questionnaire construction and pre-testing, sampling, interviewing, editing and coding, tabulation, assisting in report writing
- Supervised the work of 50 people in a research project for a large data processing client. Consisted of 20,000 interviews conducted via CRT's. Resulted in significant change to client's market strategy.
- Advised study directors on design of online research studies.

Survey Programmer II

Assisted programmers in developing electronic questionnaires for the CRT. Maintained survey data and verified tabulated research results.

- Received three promotions within 11 months of hire.

B. M. Smith & Associates   Summer Practicum 1997
Study Coordinator

Responsible for conducting a research project to determine most effective type of renovation of client's shopping center. Duties included: sample and questionnaire design, collection of primary and secondary data, tabulation, interpretive analysis of data.

Marymount College of Virginia   September, 1994 to May, 1995
Study Skills Instructor

Taught study, presentation and interpersonal skills in 15-week courses to students with academic and personal problems.

Chilton Research Services   November, 1995 to August, 1996
Interviewer

Conducted telephone interviews for both consumer and industrial studies. Exceeded quota 100% of the time.

EDUCATION

BA, magna cum laude, Business Administration, Marymount College of Virginia, 1995
AA, Business Administration/General Merchandising, Marymount College of Virginia,1994

Honors and Awards:

- Selected twice for "Who's Who in American Universities."
- Vice President of Student Faculty Council for two successive years.
- Member of four honor societies

CONTINUING EDUCATION

Attended various American Marketing Association seminars on market research techniques, as well as courses on written communication.

OUTSIDE ACTIVITIES

Television, Radio and Advertising Club (TRAC)
Designed and conducted 1998 membership study.

Network of Women in Computer Technology (NWCT)
Designed and conducted 1999 membership study.

LILLIAN LOWANS

43 Marlborough Lane
North Orange, New Jersey 07999
(908) 555-1111

Summary of Qualifications

Four years of executive secretarial experience coupled with continuing college education. A solid history of excellent work relationships, both with the public and with internal personnel at all organizational levels. High in initiative and energy with strong ability to exercise independent judgment. Excellent writing skills. Trustworthy and discreet.

Professional Skills

Proficient in the use of computers: Word, Windows, Excel, Lotus 1-2-3, Powerpoint.

But more importantly, can take on major projects and handle from initiation and planning through to implementation and follow-up.

Employment History

DataPro   1996 to Present
Senior Secretary to Manager of Department

Performed general secretarial duties with minimum supervision.

- Represent manager in collecting activity reports from departmental professional staff; compile and draft final report for signature.
- Compose letters independently or from general direction as required.
- Administer the entire *Competitive Information System* from receipt of information through acknowledgement, analysis flow, publicity and final entry into the computer system.
- Maintain and monitor correspondence/communication follow-up system.
- Monitor status of departmental projects.
- Supervise temporary typists.

Intercounty Savings Association   1994 to 1996
Executive Secretary to President

Performed general secretarial/administrative duties and coordinated all personal and business affairs of the president.

- Acted as liaison between president and branch offices, as well as service corporations, the general public, insurance companies, government agencies and members of the U.S. Senate and the House of Representatives.
- Calculated daily subsidiary figures to allow determination of funds flow. Based on the outcome, wired and borrowed funds.
- Prepared minutes for Board of Directors and committee meetings.
- Solicited bids and handled insurance for Association and personnel to comply with federal guidelines. Maintained approximately 100 personnel records.
- Distributed and administered travelers checks and U.S. Government savings bonds for all branches.

Yarway Corporation   **1991 to 1994**
Secretary to Manager of Manufacturing/Plant Engineering   1992 to 1994

Performed a variety of secretarial duties with little supervision.

- Directed the work flow through the department and supervised a full-time clerk.

- Collected, analyzed and assembled data from reports and print-outs into meaningful logs and charts for manager's use.

- Coordinated the flow of blueprint adaptations to obtain bids for the manufacturing of special tooling.

- Handled a variety of projects at the request of manager.

Assistant to Secretary of Vice President of Manufacturing   June, 1991 to May, 1992
and President of Yarway North American Division

Typed large volumes of correspondence and reports in a timely fashion; distributed reports; updated manuals, including the *Quality Assurance Manual* for the ASME; performed general clerical duties.

Cost Accounting Clerk (part-time, work/study program)   September, 1981 to June, 1982

Analyzed routings to determine individual costs of labor and material; posted figures; and assisted other members of the Accounting Department in routing accounting functions.

EDUCATION

Plymouth Whitemarsh Senior High School, Whitemarsh, PA
Graduated Class of 1991. Business Major, Work/Study Program

SUPPLEMENTAL EDUCATION (Most recent)

Basic Principles of Supervisory Management, Work Organization, Time Management,
Improving Management Skills of Secretaries, and
Various Computer Courses

Résumés for People with "Nothing to Offer"

One's prime is elusive . . .
You must be on the alert to recognize
your prime at whatever time of life it may occur.
Muriel Spark, *The Prime of Miss Jean Brodie*

Recent college graduates, homemakers or those with very little or very low-level work experience often feel as though they have nothing to offer. They say: "Kate, if I had the experience the people in your examples had, I'd have no trouble writing a résumé."

These people are wrong in a number of ways:

1. Even the highest-level executives have a great deal of difficulty figuring out what their accomplishments have been and preparing their own résumés. Résumé preparation is a skill just as marketing or finance is a skill and it is not something executives need to do every day on their jobs.

2. You are not competing with high-powered executives. Therefore, it doesn't matter that you haven't run a division of 600 people. If you had run that division, you'd have other problems in preparing your résumé.

3. It's better for each of us, no matter what our experiences, to cultivate a positive outlook: to assure ourselves that we have done okay, despite mistakes and wrong turns. Our experiences have made us what we are today and that's not so bad. We should be proud of whoever we are and make the most of it. We should each strive—executive, young person, homemaker—to uncover our special gifts and contributions and let the world know.

On a national TV program, I was once asked to work with an "ordinary housewife" and develop a résumé for her. It was promoted as something akin to magic. Can Kate make this nothing into a something? The producers picked someone who had been at home for twenty years. That would be a good one! Without even seeing her (which increased the illusion of magic), I interviewed the woman and developed a great résumé for her.

Afterwards, the people who worked in the studio said it wasn't fair: we should have picked someone who *really* had nothing to offer. They were convinced that a typical "ordinary housewife" could not possibly have an interesting résumé. These studio executives were voicing a prejudice that reinforces the way many people feel about themselves.

I was successful with the "ordinary housewife" because, in real life, most homemakers are *not* sitting home doing nothing for twenty years. A career counselor can help find the things anyone has to offer. Every homemaker and every young person has *done things*. With an open mind and the right help, these can be presented well in a résumé.

The Process

Prior to show time, I spent one hour on the phone with Maria, with no preparation on her part. You, however, would be wise to prepare by doing some of the exercises listed below. If you have trouble doing them, don't worry. You can do them with your counselor.

1. **List the fields you think you would like to go into**. If you have a clear idea about what you want to do in the future, that's great. Even if you don't, you can still have a fine résumé.

2. **List all the work you have ever done** before your marriage (or school) or during it. It does not matter whether you earned money doing this work. For example, Maria "helped out" in her daughter's store. She didn't get paid for it, but it added a lot to her résumé.

3. **List all the volunteer work you have ever done** for your place of worship, school, neighbors and friends. What are the things you find yourself doing again and again? For example, do you find you are always baking cakes for parties, babysitting or volunteering to tutor? List these things.

4. **List any organizations you have belonged to and any courses you have taken.**

5. **List your most important personality traits**. Are your detail-oriented? Are you able to motivate others? Do you follow through on everything you tackle?

6. **List your favorite hobbies, pastimes or interests**. Perhaps, for example, you enjoy needlepoint. I had one client whose passion was bowling—she not only bowled but she also scheduled tournaments. We were able to make a résumé out of it, and she got a job with a bowling association!

Try to list everything, no matter how silly it seems. Then **set up an appointment with your counselor**.

These are essentially the same exercises top executives do. Again, the Seven Stories Exercise is the key to uncovering those things you enjoyed doing and also did well—and would like to do again. And the exercise is helpful in uncovering other things as well. Through the exercise, you will find out:

• what you have done that you are proud of. In the sample résumés that follow, each person has found something to be proud of, whether it's earning money to go through school or helping a daughter in her shop.

• personality traits that will separate you from the competition, such as the ones noted in the summary statement of Larry's résumé which follows: productive, self-motivated, and so on.

• how to look at your work, school and volunteer experience objectively. In Larry's example, he spent a great deal of time analyzing the job he had. This analysis gave his résumé a lot of substance.

Even young people with no "real" work experience, or housewives who have been out of the workforce a long while can develop strong résumés—if they can think about their experiences objectively.

And, as with executives, the experiences have to be "repositioned" to fit the target market. For example, Maria said she had helped her daughter in the store. The fact is, Maria was alone in the store a lot of the time. Therefore, she was "managing the store." And when she went shopping with her daughter for things to sell in the store, they were not "shopping" but "buying."

Give it a try. With a little help and an open mind, you too can develop a résumé that truly reflects you.

LAWRENCE A. DiCAPPA
1112 Vermont Lane
Downingtown, PA
(215) 555-1111

SUMMARY OF QUALIFICATIONS

Extensive product knowledge is coupled with creative ideas for product applications and a solid history of sales success. A proven ability to develop sales potential in new market areas. Strong analytical and planning skills, combined with the ability to coordinate the efforts of many to meet organizational goals. Productive and efficient work habits without supervision. Self-motivator and high energy.

PROFESSIONAL EXPERIENCE

A solid background in sales and product experience.
Additional supervisory as well as training experience.

EMPLOYMENT HISTORY

Telephone Sales Representative, AMP Special Industries   June, 1994-Present

o Achieved 140% growth in assigned account responsibility: from $90,000 to $230,000 in the year 1995. Accounts were previously declining at 35% annually.

o Developed a complete marketing program where none previously existed. Program now serves as a guide for new hires and future departmental growth.

o Set up and established new territory by:

- Devising a technique for introducing the sales concept and then the product to customers.

- Designing an introductory call script which is now a standard for the department.

- Developing a strategy for attacking and penetrating a customer master list.

- Serving as product specialist and trainer for six new hires.

- Developing complete managerial outline for continued growth and success of the department.

o Finished in top three in both advanced and basic sales training classes.

DiCAPPA

EMPLOYMENT HISTORY, contd.

Office Manager, American Excelsior Company   1990 to 1994
  (approximately two years full-time while attending college)

  o Responsible for internal sales service.

  o Purchased 70% of company's raw materials.

  o Managed work flow for an office of five personnel.

  o Coordinated the workload of warehouse and trucking personnel in
    arranging shipments of customer orders via company-owned fleet and common
    carriers.

EDUCATION

BS, Business Administration, Drexel University, Philadelphia, PA, 1994
  Major: Marketing, 4.0 average in field of concentration.

  65% of total college expenses were earned through full-time and part-time employment.

Homemaker's Résumé

1234 'XYZ' Street
City, State 11999
515-555-3456

Summary of Qualifications

The most important highlight of your experience is placed first. This is followed by your other experiences and skills. Perhaps you are an excellent administrator or organizer, work well with all kinds of people, or have some other special experience. The counselor will help determine the best way to express your strengths.

Professional Experience

Job Title or function you performed   dates or years
Company or organization name or project you worked on

- Here are listed some of the things you did there.
- **Think about what you *really* did, whether or not it was your job to do it**.
- It is *very* difficult to think about these things yourself. A career counselor is able to develop a résumé that reflects your experience. Your résumé will look like this one.

Another Job Title or function you performed   dates or years
Company or organization name or project you worked on

- A list of the things you did, **whether or not you were paid for them.**
- If the work you did was not for an organization, but was for family or friends, that's okay. We can make a résumé out of those experiences also.

PTA   1976 to present

- Maria thought her PTA experience was useless. But we expressed what she had done in a way that reflected her efforts. We can do the same for you. Do *not* compare your experiences to Maria's. Comparing yourself to someone else will prevent you from thinking about those things you truly did well, enjoyed doing, and are proud of.

- Instead, **think only about yourself**: What do *you* enjoy doing? What are you good at? What do you find yourself doing again and again? Do you find yourself "catering" parties for friends? Then, let's talk about it. Do you stage raffles for your church or synagogue? Let's talk about it. Have you held posts in an organization? What do others say about your work? What do *you* think about your work? Let's talk about it, and put it down on paper.

- I know you are proud of your husband and children. But instead of telling me about their accomplishments, tell me about yours. This may be difficult for you because you may be used to building them up instead of yourself. But we are not trying to get *them* a job. We're trying to get *you* a job, and so we have to talk about you and how good you are. Let's give it a try. Believe it or not, *everyone* comes out with a good résumé.

Coursework

We'll list here any courses you have taken if they are appropriate.

Maria Salerno

4756 Cashew Lane
Sweet Briar, Missouri 99000
999-555-3456

Summary of Qualifications

9 years' experience in office management and the fashion industry. 10 years as an officer or committee member for a not-for-profit organization. A thorough, conscientious and hard worker who meets deadlines and gets the job done. Works well with others including management, peers and the public.

Professional Experience

Salesperson/Store Manager (Part-time)   1-1/2 years
Propaganda Boutique, **(top-of-the-line women's clothing)**

- As Assistant Buyer, went to showrooms, selected clothing and accessories.
- Managed the store. Dealt with the public. Handled complaints.

Office Manager   3 years
Micro-Ohm Corporation
Office Manager for a 30-person company.

- Kept books, did the payroll, answered the phones.
- Regular contact with clients and employees. Worked closely with the President.

Bookkeeping Department
Lansing Knitwear (Also modeled clothing)   2 years
Chase Manhattan Bank   3 years

PTA   1976 to present

Over the course of 13 years, served as Vice President and on every Committee.
- Received **Certificate of Appreciation** for outstanding service and dedication.

- As **Vice President** (2 years),
   - Substituted for the President. Attended the Board meetings of all Committees.

- With members of the **International Committee,**
   - **Researched foreign countries**. Visited consulates. Recruited speakers.
   - **Held special events** to represent each country to the students. Served foreign foods, handed out flags, had dancers, or did whatever else was appropriate for that country.

- As a member of other committees,
   - **Recruited various speakers** to address the students.
   - These included a nutritionist, a computer expert, a Chinese cook, experts on drug and alcohol abuse, and so on. Also had **State senators and representatives** come in to address parents' concerns.

- As PTA Liaison, regularly meet with the Principal, Department Heads, and faculty members. Meetings are held to update the PTA, and to ask questions of the faculty.
- Serve as a delegate to other schools as a representative of the PTA.

Fluent in Italian; Familiar with Spanish.

PART EIGHT

JUMP-START FOR NEW GRADS

The Five O'Clock Club®

Jump-Start for New Grads

by Mark Gonska

Graduation Day. Long speeches that inspire yawns from the crowd. The march begins, names are called, a few cut-ups do cartwheels on the stage, degrees are conferred. Cheers, congratulations, champagne. School is finally over. Look out, world . . . Here I come.

But where do I go?

The classified ads read:

"IS PROFESSIONAL - ideal candidate will have 3+ years of experience with UNIX, TCP/IP, Novell, OS/2 . . . "

"ATTORNEY - 3-5 years litigation experience (minimum) . . . "

"ACCOUNTANT - manufacturer requires accountant with minimum 2 years experience with month-end closings, account analysis, PC applications . . . "

Today, educational credentials alone are not enough. Recent graduates of all ages, who have degrees in many different disciplines, are stalled before their careers even start. After months of job hunting, they settle for a job outside of their chosen field. They are frustrated. Embarrassed. Disenchanted. Parents and friends watch from the sidelines and wish they could help.

The central theme of The Five O'Clock Club is a determination to deal with the toughest challenges facing job hunters and career changers. The Club targets the real issues that others would rather avoid.

Some job searches are relatively simple and can yield some amazing opportunities in a short period of time. The job seeker who is in demand, who has demonstrated skills and an extensive background for the hottest job markets, is "easy"

to help through the process. In fact, the counselor may spend more time advising *against* taking the wrong offer and focus on evaluating the best of the "six to ten things in the works."

Countless job-hunting books are available for so-called easy job searches. But here is a tough search:

How Do You Get Your First "Real" Job When You Have Limited Experience or None?

If so many potential employers want one to two years of experience before they will hire a candidate, even for an entry-level job, where does the experience come from?

Few employers will spend the time or money that is required to train new employees. They want players who can "hit the ground running," based on an exact match of previous experience with the job in question.

Therefore, the best time to get the experience is *before* graduation.

High School

For many years, there were two main tracks to run on in the United States:

1. The college preparatory track was for the brightest or most socially acceptable kids. These students were expected to survive based on their ability to think.

2. The vocational track was for those considered to be better with their hands than their heads. These students learned a trade. They were trained to develop skills employers or customers would be willing to pay for.

Today, the lines between these two tracks are blurred. The white-collar college tracker faces the challenge to demonstrate specific skills, to produce tangible results and to increase corporate profit.

The hands-on vocational tracker must also bring added value to the employer. Production is aided by automation and advanced technology. The traditional blue-collar worker must show that he or she can think beyond the confines of the mechanized production line, computer-aided design package, robotics or integrated software package.

The roles are blended further as the white-collar employee must produce, not just think, and the blue-collar worker must think, not just produce.

With these pressures, the exercises in Part Two: "Deciding What You Want" in *Targeting the Job You Want* are essential for job seekers of the future.

Even a high school junior could benefit from completing the Seven Stories exercises. Examining the Skills and Interests section could be particularly helpful to young people. In addition, the Forty-Year Vision can be an incredible tool. With the help of a parent or other counselor, the high school student can identify up to three potential career targets.

The outline below could be completed by a high school student in preparation for college or a vocational/apprentice program.

During High School

A. Identify Job Target 1: _____

B. Here are three people I know of who work in this job area now:
    1. _____
    2. _____
    3. _____

C. Here are some questions to ask them:
    1. What do you like best about your job?
    2. What do you like least about your job?
    3. What do you think the market for your type of job will be in five years?
    4. What new skills will be necessary by then?
    5. Where did you go to school?
    6. What was your major?
    7. What part of your education has been most valuable in your job?
    8. What trade or professional journals or magazines do you read?
    9. What are the most important professional or industry associations in your field?
    10. Would you encourage your son/daughter to enter your field? Why or why not?
    11. Does your company ever have internships?
    12. Who is the top human resources person in your company?
    13. Who are your best competitors?
    14. Where do you see yourself in five years?
    15. Where is the best place to start in this business?

This outline should be completed for Job Targets 2 and 3 as well.

D. Keep in touch with these people, by phone or by mail, on a quarterly basis.

E. Based on my interviews, here are the main categories of courses that would seem most valuable for my target positions.

_____
_____
_____
_____

F. Based on my interviews, here are some additional courses that would broaden my understanding of Target 1 or would just be fun.

_____
_____
_____
_____

G. Internships, study topics, life experiences and other information I would want to make sure I have on my résumé before I graduate from college or vocational/apprentice program:

_____
_____
_____
_____

H. Potential Colleges/Training Programs/Apprenticeships for Target 1:

_____
_____
_____

I. People I know who attend these schools now:

_____
_____
_____

I believe the true road to preeminent success in any line is to make
yourself master of that line.
Andrew Carnegie

J.   What can the department heads tell me about internship programs or post-graduate success stories?

_____

_____

_____

_____

K.   Here is what I'd like my résumé to look like when I graduate:

_____

_____

_____

_____

Post High School (Think Internship First, Tuition Scholarship Second)

Today, the costs associated with completing a typical bachelor's degree are approaching six figures. Incredible sacrifices are made by students, parents and financial institutions in order to secure these huge sums.

Few investors would risk this much money without subjecting their investment to a thorough investigation. You wouldn't buy a sub sandwich business if you had never been inside a sub sandwich shop or tasted the product, would you? Before buying the business you might first work in a sub shop, perhaps even for minimum wage. Only then would you be willing to invest your money.

Even if you could afford to squander four or five years' worth of tuition money, consider the opportunities lost if you spent time and energy in a college or advanced training program that didn't quite fit.

Employers today are selective. The costs of hiring the right employee and the costs of legally terminating the wrong one are steadily increasing. Understandably, more employers are now scrutinizing credentials for new hires.

Nothing speaks more loudly to potential employers than practical experience, paid or unpaid, in your desired field. Many successful people began their careers with humble, thankless jobs. Work ethic, character and perseverance can be developed by mopping floors, crewing for a fast-food restaurant or running the vacuum cleaner at a Barnes & Noble. But there is another way.

Consider volunteering to work in your Target 1 field. Many so-called internships start off that way, and the experience gained is invaluable. Internship-type opportunities should be investigated *before* you enroll in them. Never mind the assurances that good things are bound to happen in a junior, senior or fifth year.

Get the facts from people who are in the internship programs now. Talk with the interns and company representatives and get names. Do your investigating before enrolling.

During College or Advanced Training: Begin with the End in Mind

Write the résumé you would like to present to your first post-graduation employer. Include jobs you have already had, the experience you would like to obtain and other goals you would like to achieve.

At the beginning of every quarter, review your "resume of the future" before you select your classes. Keep this résumé in a highly visible place. It's a great conversation starter.

College planning is not a contradiction in terms. Beyond the course curriculum, strategic thinking is required. The career services center on campus is a key resource; take time to establish a relationship with the director. Volunteer or get a paid position in career services to learn how to maximize the benefits from this office.

Learn who is responsible for internships and work/study arrangements with outside corporations in the local community. Do not wait for others to hand you an internship. Learn how to get one yourself. Also, school administrators are proud to speak of graduates who have become success stories. Ask for alumni who are working in your chosen field and contact them.

Which individuals and corporations donate funds to the school? There may be opportunities to capitalize on these connections. Why not volunteer in the development office? From the inside, you may be able to investigate companies in your chosen field. After all, they are potential donors. Imagine the value of meeting with senior executives from companies in your target fields. By positioning yourself properly before graduation, you can distinguish yourself from thousands of others.

Targets for an Attorney: Sarah Moghal

Sarah Moghal came from a family of professionals. Her father, a general surgeon, had built up a strong practice through forty years of hard work. With that same kind of work ethic and determination, Sarah completed her undergraduate degree.

For Sarah, entering law school brought with it excitement and dreams of righting the wrongs of society. Her summers were filled with law clerk positions at local firms. Graduating from law school meant more grueling hours of study for Sarah to pass the bar exam and become admitted to the state Bar.

Then the realities of supply and demand came into focus. There are lots of attorneys. More are graduating every semester. However, the demand for legal services does not seem to be growing as quickly.

Sarah selected prime opportunities posted at her law school placement office. She sent out résumés and hoped for the best. She subscribed to the *Ohio Bar Association Report (OBAR)*, which serves as a clearinghouse for classified ads for admitted attorneys. She answered ads.

Most advertisements failed to result in even a rejection letter, let alone an offer. She worked harder and answered more ads, even for positions that she felt were beneath her.

Sarah finally landed a part-time job with a small firm. Much of the work she received seemed to be at the law clerk level, similar to the summer jobs she had held for the last three years. The pay was not significantly better.

Sarah became part of the "underground" of underemployed professionals. Many capable people in every market have settled for part-time jobs, sometimes outside their chosen fields. They are stuck and unsure of what to do next.

The Five O'Clock Club approach is an important tool job searchers can use to get unstuck. Sarah went through the assessment exercises in *Targeting the Job You Want* and identified three job targets. She had not received any significant offers while playing the generalist role. Yet, the idea of focusing on specific targets seemed like wishful thinking to Sarah, at least initially. She was concerned that "pigeon-holing" her approach would limit her options even further.

Despite her concerns, The Five O'Clock Club approach eventually came to make sense to her. Anything productive would be an improvement.

Sarah's initial résumé was designed using the format recommended by her law school. It looked nearly identical to those of hundreds of other newly graduated lawyers—a juris doctor degree, summer clerk experience and little else.

Sarah identified three targets:

Target 1:
    Industry: Public Sector
    Position: Municipal Law
    Geographic area: Cleveland

Target 2:
    Industry: Local Firm
    Position: Staff Attorney Specializing in Municipal Law
    Geographic area: Cleveland

Target 3:
    Industry: Public Sector
    Position: Municipal Law
    Geographic area: Chicago

Discussions with Sarah revealed that she had had a fair amount of experience with municipal law. In fact, the firm where she had clerked and now worked as an attorney had served as a kind of law department for five city governments. The significance of the firm had to be highlighted on her résumé. Also, an accurate description of the types of municipal casework she had done was essential.

Sarah's "after" résumé is two pages ahead.

SARAH N. MOGHAL
6662 Gates Mills Blvd.
Gates Mills, OH 44040
(216) 555-0820

EDUCATION: **Cleveland-Marshall College of Law**
Cleveland, Ohio
J.D., 1998
<u>Business Law Classes</u>: Commecial (sic) Law; Secured Transactions; Real Estate;
Small Business Enterprises; Antitrust
GPA: 3.43/4.00

Ohio State University
Columbus, Ohio
B. S. in Business Administration, 1995
<u>Major</u>: Finance
GPA: 3.80/4.0

WORK EXPERIENCE:

January 1999-
Present

Robert J. Dobbs Jr. & Associates
(AV-Rated) Cleveland, Ohio (216) 555-1567
<u>Attorney</u>. Handle cases in the areas of *commercial contracts, business, municipal, labor and personal injury law*. Perform research, drafting of briefs, pleadings and interrogatories; debtor's exams, depositions, litigation support, court appearances.

February 1998 -
May 1998

Chadbourne & Lewis
Cleveland, Ohio (216) 999-5500
<u>Law Clerk</u>. Performed legal research and wrote memoranda in the areas of *consumer sales* and *personal injury*, drafted pleadings.

Summer 1997

Jerome and Zoller
Cleveland, Ohio (216) 533-2200
<u>Law Clerk</u>. Conducted legal research and wrote memoranda in the areas of *business law* and *contracts*; filed pleadings.

Summer 1996

Uhlinger and Keis
Cleveland, Ohio (216) 681-4100
<u>Law Clerk</u>. Provided legal research in the areas of *torts*, *contracts* and *insurance subrogation*; prepared complaints; wrote legal memoranda.

BAR ADMISSION: State Bar of Ohio, 1998; Member, American Bar Association; Member, Ohio State Bar Association; Member, Cleveland Bar Association.

PERSONAL: Proficient with LEXIS, WESTLAW, and numerous word processing programs. Knowledge of Lotus. Enjoy basketball and reading.

SARAH N. MOGHAL, ESQ.
6662 Gates Mills Boulevard
Gates Mills, Ohio 44040
(216) 555-0820[H]; (216) 555-6800[O]

MUNICIPAL LAW ATTORNEY

with the research, analytical and writing skills required to provide timely opinions and interpretations. Accustomed to meeting stringent deadlines. Experience includes:

- Legislative Analysis
- Tort Liability/Sovereign Immunity
- Contract/Liability Issues

- Zoning Interpretation
- Employment Litigation
- Land Usage

Employment History

Attorney   1999 to Present
ROBERT J. DOBBS, JR. & ASSOCIATES, Cleveland, Ohio
[An AV-Rated firm serving as legal department/prosecutor for five municipalities.]

- Support litigation involving all aspects of municipal law.
- Assist with complex cases; gained broad experience with labor and commercial contract disputes.
- Participated in successful litigation of a major suit involving vindication of employee's rights.
- Research, prepare and draft pleadings, motions briefs and memoranda of law; execute all phases of discovery.
- Completed research and wrote opinions on municipal legislation, zoning variances, traffic law, taxation and land usage cases.

Law Clerk   1996 - 1998
CHADBOURNE & LEWIS (1998)

- Conducted research, organized and wrote legal memoranda, drafted complaints and briefs involving the Ohio Consumer Sales Practices Act and personal injury cases.

JEROME AND ZOLLER (1997)

- Provided legal research and drafted memoranda regarding business organizations, anti-competitive practices and contracts.

UHLINGER AND KEIS (Summer, 1996)

- Researched, wrote memoranda and drafted pleadings on personal injury and insurance subrogation issues.

Education and Training

JD, Cleveland-Marshall College of Law, 1998
BS, Business Administration, The Ohio State University, 1995 (Major: Finance)

Proficient with LEXIS, WESTLAW, word processing and spreadsheet applications.

Bar Admission

State Bar of Ohio, 1998
Member: American Bar Association, Ohio State Bar Association, Cleveland Bar Association

Words have weight, sound and appearance; it is only by considering these that you can write a sentence that is good to look at and good to listen to.
W. Somerset Maugham

What Sarah Did Next
Target 1, a position in her local city's law department.

Like most public sector situations, the hiring process for Sarah's first target was mired in red tape, multiple gatekeepers and delays. But Sarah was persistent. She found a decision-maker and arranged for a personal interview. During the meeting, she positioned herself in light of her updated pitch for municipal law. She also identified two "influencers" in the prosecutor's office and met with them for advice. Unfortunately, the meeting with the Law Director was delayed twice.

In the process, Target 3, a position in Chicago's law department, came into play. Sarah contacted The Five O'Clock Club affiliate in Chicago for some help with local firms that specialized in municipal law. One of the leads she got resulted in a job offer with an attorney who was planning to leave an established firm. The soon-to-be entrepreneur needed a young attorney to help him hit the ground running. The stories of how the initial long hours of work would turn to gold were music to Sarah's ears.

However, Sarah declined the offer. She really needed structure, training and a mentor, none of which this start-up opportunity would provide. While she was in Chicago, Sarah did the unthinkable. She walked into the city's law offices and asked to meet with the Law Director. No appointment, no previous résumé, letter or contact of any kind. She claimed that she had only one afternoon in Chicago and needed only a few minutes to meet with the director. She asked for help.

After a forty-minute wait, Sarah was ushered into the office. She had rehearsed the questions she needed to ask. During a short but cordial reception, Sarah met the director, presented her pitch and received important advice on how to navigate through the departmental bureaucracy.

She felt that prospects were encouraging enough to study for the Illinois Bar Exam. After careful consideration, she feels that relocating to Chicago is the preferred option. Despite an abundance of law schools and a plethora of attorneys there, Sarah sees greater opportunity in the Chicago market. Currently, Sarah is spending most of her waking hours studying for the Illinois Bar. Despite this decision, she is still pursuing Targets 1 and 2.

Accounting for All of Your Skills: Ismail Daod.

While capturing a job when you have limited experience is difficult under the best circumstances, additional issues like age, disability, gender and national origin can present further challenges. Regardless of the Equal Employment Opportunity Commission, these biases persist. While some of these differences can actually be an asset in certain environments, they need to be handled carefully.

Concerned about his Middle Eastern accent, Ismail Daod wondered if his lack of interviews was due to discrimination. Were his first words on the telephone revealing his ethnic background and immediately disqualifying him? His frustration led him to do the worst thing any job seeker can do: nothing. Ismail stopped making follow-up phone calls, and started feeling sorry for himself. He wondered if the thousands of dollars and hundreds of hours he had invested in his accounting degree had all been a waste.

In a desperate frame of mind, he met with his Five O'Clock Club coach. The coach recommended a different approach: to think of the accent as an asset rather than as a liability. The idea sounded ridiculous to Ismail. He developed thirty-second and two-minute pitches that actually emphasized Ismail's ethnic background. Ismail was skeptical, but he felt that his situation couldn't get any worse.

Target 1 was made up of small to midsize public accounting firms that served local businesses owned by Arab-Americans. The Five O'Clock Club coach recommended that he contact a high-profile city councilman of Arabic descent. The councilman told Ismail about two professional organizations made up of Target 1 businesses. He also provided Ismail with current membership rosters of each association.

172

ISMAIL A. DAOD
1120 Revere Drive
Glenfield, Ohio 44113
(216) 888-4160

OBJECTIVE Desire to positively contribute my diverse entrepreneurial skills to an accounting establishment that needs an analytical, hardworking and resourceful person.

SUMMARY Strong background in purchasing, supply and negotiations. Experience with Lotus. Excellent customer service skills; an accomplished entrepreneur. Bilingual (English and Arabic) and enjoy traveling.

EMPLOYMENT

CAVANAGH ACCOUNTING, Cleveland, Ohio   (11/98-Present)
Accounting Staff
Prepare payroll
Prepare sales taxes and returns
Check compliance with local and federal regulations.

A & I INC., Cleveland, Ohio   (1996-Present)
President
Oversee all bookkeeping matters
Ensure compliance with all relevant tax regulations
Increase net worth of corporation from $2,000 to $100,000 in 3 years.

3M, Cleveland, Ohio   (2/93-3/96)
Salesman
Conducted 50-60% of division sales.

MIKE DISCOUNTS, Cleveland, Ohio   (1990-1993)
Section Manager, Dairy & Frozen Section
Department Manager
Managed a chain of 10 stores
Ordered and stocked commodities.

EDUCATION Cleveland State University, Cleveland, Ohio
Bachelor's of Business Administration, March 1998
Major: Accounting
Major GPA: 3.38/4.0
CPA Candidate.

Amman Community College
Diploma, 1989
Major: Business and Office Practice
Took Jordan Comprehensive Professional Examination
and was rated fifth best candidate in the country.

ACTIVITIES Member, Cleveland State University Accounting Association.
Running, swimming, travel.

References will be provided upon request.

ISMAIL A. DAOD

1120 Revere Drive, Glenfield, Ohio 44113   (216) 888-4160

ACCOUNTING PROFESSIONAL
Diverse analytical skills, proven business sense and technical expertise.

- Financial analysis
- Efficiency enhancements
- Multiple software packages
- Operational controls
- Cash management
- Tax preparation and filing

Summary of Related Experience:

Productivity: Established a reputation for effectiveness and efficiency; able to complete assignments on time and within budget. Demonstrated an exceptional energy level and strong negotiating skills. Managed multiple projects and departmental responsibility.

Financial Analysis: Gained experience in business analysis, valuation and acquisition.

System Enhancements: Provided more effective internal management reporting. Constructed and analyzed financial reports using Lotus 1-2-3 spreadsheets, TurboTax, QuickBooks, Quicken and many others. Understand Windows '95 and '98 operating systems.

An aggressive professional who has demonstrated determination to reach ambitious goals. Skilled in general accounting, auditing and tax planning. Passed the CPA exam in May 1995.

Staff Accountant, CAVANAGH ACCOUNTING SERVICES, Cleveland, Ohio   1998 to Present
- Prepare payroll and sales tax filings for over 50 businesses. File corporate taxes.
- Construct financial reports. Provide full-charge bookkeeping through financial statements.
- Assure compliance with tax regulations.
- Advise clients on investment options, performance enhancement, asset allocation strategies and risk management.

Principal, A & I INC., Cleveland, Ohio   1996 to 1998
- Established a successful business. Starting with an undergraduate class project, recognized a real-world opportunity and now participate in a business with a six-figure net worth.
- Created, constructed and implemented all financial reporting and operational controls.
- Learned, hands-on, how to manage inventory and maximize cash flow.

Sales Representative, 3M Distribution Company, Cleveland, Ohio   1993 to 1996
- Ranked as top sales producer among six sales representatives. Negotiated sales agreements.

Department Manager, Mike Discounts, Cleveland, Ohio   1990 to 1993
- Managed a chain of 10 stores.

EDUCATION AND PROFESSIONAL TRAINING

BBA, Accounting, Cleveland State University, 1998 (GPA: 3.38/4.0 in major); CPA candidate

Jordan Comprehensive Professional Examination
Rated as the country's fifth best accounting candidate.

Proud U. S. citizen; Open to travel

Whenever you can, shorten a sentence. And one always can. . . .
Caress your sentence tenderly; it will end by smiling at you.
Anatole France

Ismail scripted out a thirty-second pitch and then contacted these business owners by telephone. The pitch went something like this:

"I am an Arab-American with proven business start-up and management experience. I have built on this hands-on experience by completing accounting and CPA training. My lifelong goal has been to better serve the Arab-American business community. Specifically, I want to join an accounting firm that has demonstrated a commitment to this growing ethnic group. I am willing to start at a lower position and work toward using my business skills and accounting training to help others overcome the obstacles I have faced in obtaining financing, implementing prudent financial controls and reducing unnecessary taxation. Further, I bring a personal understanding of cross-cultural challenges as well as multiple language skills."

More than once, Ismail delivered his thirty-second pitch in Arabic. Each contact could prove to be an important resource. For Target 2, Ismail hoped to join an Arab-American-owned company as an accountant or financial manager.

Five O'Clock Club research indicates that follow-up phone calls require an average of eight attempts to actually reach the desired contact. Therefore, to reach his forty targeted companies, Ismail might need to make more than 300 telephone calls. So far, the hard work has paid off handsomely. In two months, he has already generated seven face-to-face interviews.

Ismail also learned about three smaller accounting firms that cater to Arab-American clients and he has received additional requests to help with year-end financial reporting. Most importantly, when Ismail put the accent on his strengths and began marketing himself more effectively, he found a much more receptive audience. His pitch worked, not because of any clever trick or technique, but because he used the Five O'Clock Club method to determine what he really wanted to do. His sincerity would have come through in any language.

A Professional Track—
Instead of a Job in Fast-Food: Shelley

Many young people feel stuck in the fast food jungle and are unsure of how to prevent the phrase "would you like fries with your order" from being permanently etched into their memories. Real-world experience would sure be an improvement over hokey uniforms and bussing tables. Yet, how does a young person acquire real-world experience, and is it possible to get *before* completing a degree program? Can young people be prepositioned, that is, put on their career track before completing their degree, in a technical field that requires professional licensing? With rapid, profound change affecting so many professions, how can anyone identify a career path that offers sustained growth?

Shelley Mulligan, a high-school student from Ohio, wanted to pursue a career in nursing. Her friends and family thought Shelley had overlooked the headlines. The local hospital market was consolidating. Two of the area's largest hospitals had merged, and experienced nurses were let go in the ensuing "streamlining" and downsizing. Rumors that other hospitals would be closing became reality as major health care consortiums swallowed up the strongest remaining facilities. What would a national health care plan mean for nurses? What would the job market look like when Shelley finished her degree?

Despite these valid concerns, Shelley insisted that nursing was her calling. She worked with a Five O'Clock Club counselor to devise a flexible career development plan to better position her for the future. The assumptions made in this plan were debatable but seemed to make sense:

- Health care delivery systems will continue to consolidate and change at an accelerated pace.

- Regardless of the changes, more services will be delivered on an outpatient basis.

- Home health care options will expand and continue to displace traditional hospital employment opportunities.

- Lower-level technicians will perform more support work and further reduce the demand for traditional RN staffing.
- Specialization and advanced training will be a requirement for the professional nurse in the U.S.
- People will live longer; older people will make up a larger percentage of the U.S. population. All aspects of eldercare and geriatrics will be in greater demand in the future.
- Developing countries will have an unfilled demand and will lack funding for health care professionals.

This was serious analysis for a teenager, but then again Shelley was serious. She developed a career plan that focused on obtaining real experience in the hotter areas of health care , which would better weather the storms of change.

At age 17, Shelley left the fast-food crew behind and looked at food service or dietary positions in the area's upscale assisted living center. Far more than a nursing home, this facility offered many different opportunities for health care professionals. However, the most critical need at the retirement community was not for dieticians' assistants but for nurse's aides. This often thankless job is on the lowest rung of the staff hierarchy and consequently, many health care facilities suffer from a high rate of turnover among their nurse's aides. Shelley found that a $100 bonus was offered for candidates who joined the staff and completed state certification requirements. After she completed the training program—at full pay—she received an hourly increase and a shift differential bonus. Additional training and certification in CPR was also provided. Since reliable employees were so hard to find, Shelley was soon called on to work as much overtime as she was willing to take. She worked closely with the staff nurses and demonstrated a positive, enthusiastic outlook.

Before joining the staff at the retirement community, Shelley's favorite nurse had worked with a home health care service. The nurse explained that the service was always looking for nurse's aides. Shelley found that although the service did not offer benefits, they did pay 2 dollars more per hour. She liked getting out of the confines of the assisted living center and enjoyed spending more time with each patient.

In her spare time, Shelley volunteered to work at the office of her family physician. She worked there only a few hours a week, but she gained a working knowledge of the ICD-9 codes and CPT codes required for every insurance company claim. That isn't all she hoped to gain. Ever the strategist, Shelley thought that working in a physician's practice adjacent to the hospital might eventually give her a leg up on support positions within the hospital.

The next summer, Shelley put all her work responsibilities on hold for a three-week visit to Quito, Ecuador. She wanted to know what living in another culture was like, and she hoped to get a glimpse of health care outside the comforts of the U.S. The Ecuador experience gave her real inspiration and a dream to practice cross-cultural nursing.

Within eighteen months of leaving her fast-food job, Shelley acquired legitimate experience. More importantly, she has begun to learn how to develop contacts within her chosen field. In three years, she intends to graduate as a Registered Nurse with her first degree. While she can do nothing to guarantee job security, she is building not only her résumé but also her employability security. She is working hard, at times to the detriment of her social life, but she is moving forward toward her goals.

1. *Never use a long word where a short one will do.*
2. *If it is possible to cut out a word, always cut it out.*
3. *Never use the passive where you can use the active.*
4. *Never use a foreign phrase, a scientific word or a jargon word if you can think of an everyday English equivalent.*
5. *Break any of these rules sooner than say anything barbarous.*

George Orwell
"Politics and the English Language"

Shelley Marie Mulligan
2053 Aldersgate Drive
Fairstead Village, Ohio 44124
(216) 777-6804

OBJECTIVE

Entry-level position in health care leading to a position in **Nursing**.

PROFILE

Hardworking, enthusiastic individual with excellent communication skills.

EDUCATION

CUVAHOGA COMMUNITY COLLEGE, Cleveland, Ohio Pursuing Associate Degree - 1999
  Dean's List Spring, 1998

THE KING'S ACADEMY, Elyria, Ohio   Graduate - 1997
  Received Varsity Letter in fast-pitch softball.
  Toured three states with the drama group, "The Ambassadors."
  Actively participated in local political campaigns, SADD (Students Against Drunk Driving) and
  Student Council.

  Proficient with WordPerfect and Microsoft Office products.

EXPERIENCE

BURGER DELIGHT, Cleveland, Ohio
Crew Leader - 1996
Crew Person 1996 to 1997 (part-time)
As Crew Leader, directed a busy shift of customer service associates in a busy suburban location.
Gained thorough understanding of sanitation and cash-control procedures.

- Received "Crew Leader of the Month" award for three consecutive months.

- Assist manager with staff scheduling and training of newly hired associates.

THE GAP, Cleveland, Ohio
Sales Associate - 1996 to 1997 (part-time)

Enjoyed the challenge of delivering excellent service to discriminating customers. Encouraged
repeat business and maintained excellent cash controls.

VISION QUEST, INTERNATIONAL, Cleveland, Ohio
Software Duplication Assistant - 1995 to 1997 (part-time)

Duplicated a high volume of "shareware software" for wholesale distribution.

LANGUAGE PROFICIENCIES

Able to read, write and speak Spanish.

Shelley Marie Mulligan
2053 Aldersgate Drive
Fairstead Village, Ohio 44124
(216) 777-6804

Health care professional

Experience working in skilled nursing facilities, a physician's office
and on home health care assignments.
Certified Nurse's Aide, State of Ohio. Trained in CPR and Infant CPR.
Hardworking and enthusiastic.

Related Experience

THE GEORGIAN RETIREMENT COMMUNITY, ASSISTED LIVING CENTER
State-Certified Nurse's Aide - 1997 to present

Assist professional nursing staff with direct patient care and encouragement. Work with a variety of residents with special needs, including: Alzheimer's/dementia patients, orthopedics, and short- and long-term care. Work well with demanding residents, assist them with basic needs, hygiene and companionship.

- Manage the challenges of working alternating shifts and working productively with changing support staffs and nurses.

- Received attendance incentive award. Worked overtime as requested.

EVERGREEN HOME HEALTH SERVICES
Caregiver - 1998 (part-time)

- Traveled to patients requiring basic care. Interfaced with family members and prepared detailed records for review by staff nurses or physicians.

DR. KORNELIA BRATTON
Volunteer Office Assistant - 1997 to present (part-time)

- Gained an understanding of office practices and procedures in this growing family practice.

CREDENTIALS AND TRAINING

Certified Nurse's Aide - State of Ohio. Trained in CPR and Infant CPR.

EDUCATION

CUYAHOGA COMMUNITY COLLEGE, Cleveland, Ohio
Dean's List Spring, 1998
Pursuing Associate Degree - 1999

THE KING'S ACADEMY, Elyria, Ohio - **Graduate - 1997**
Received Varsity Letter in fast-pitch softball.
Toured three states with the drama group, "The Ambassadors."
Actively participated in local political campaigns, SADD (Students Against Drunk Driving)
and Student Council.

COMPUTER AND LANGUAGE PROFICIENCIES

Proficient with WordPerfect and Microsoft Office products. Able to read, write and speak Spanish.

PART NINE

RÉSUMÉ CHECKLIST: HOW GOOD IS YOUR RÉSUMÉ?

This is the true joy in life, the being used for a purpose recognized by yourself as a mighty one, the being thoroughly worn out before you are thrown on the scrap heap; the being a force of nature instead of a feverish selfish little clod of ailments and grievances complaining that the world will not devote itself to making you happy.
George Bernard Shaw

I know you are asking today, "How long will it take?" I come to say to you this afternoon, however difficult the moment, however frustrating the hour, it will not be long, because truth pressed to earth will rise again.
How long? Not long, because no lie can live forever.
How long? Not long, because you still reap what you sow.
How long? Not long, because the arm of the moral universe is long but it bends towards justice.
How long? Not long, 'cause mine eyes have seen the glory of the coming of the Lord, trampling out the vinyards where the grapes of wrath are stored. He has loosed the fateful lightning of his terrible swift sword. His truth is marching on.
He has sounded forth the trumpets that shall never call retreat. He is lifting up the hearts of man before His judgment seat. Oh, be swift, my soul, to answer Him. Be jubilant, my feet. Our God is marching on.
Martin Luther King, Jr.

Dear sir, Be patient toward all that is unsolved in your heart and try to love the <u>questions themselves</u> *like locked rooms and like books that are written in a very foreign tongue. Do not now seek the answers, which cannot be given you because you would not be able to live them. And the point is, to live everything.* <u>Live</u> *the questions now. Perhaps you will then gradually, without noticing it, live along some distant day into the answer. Perhaps you do carry within yourself the possibility of shaping and forming as a particularly happy and pure way of living; train yourself to it—but take whatever comes with trust, and if only it comes out of your own will, out of some need of your inmost being, take it upon yourself and hate nothing.*
Rainer Maria Rilke, *Letters to a Young Poet*

Résumé Checklist:
How Good Is Your Résumé?

1. Positioning:
- If I spend just **10 seconds** glancing at my résumé, what are the ideas/words that pop out? (specific job titles, my degrees, specific company names):

_____

- This is how I am "positioned" by my résumé. Is this how I want to be positioned for this target area? Or is this positioning a handicap for the area I am targeting?

2. Level:
- What *level* do I appear to be at? Is it easy for the reader to guess in 10 seconds what my level is? (For example, if I say I "install computer systems," I could be making anywhere from $15,000 a year to $200,000 a year.)

3. Summary Statement:
- If I have no summary statement, I am being positioned by the most recent job on my résumé. Is that how I want to be positioned?
- If I have a summary, does the very first line position me for the kind of job I want next?
  - Is this followed by a statement that elaborates on the first statement?
  - Is this followed by statements that prove how good I am or differentiate me from my likely competitors?
  - Have I included a statement or two that give the reader an indication of my personality or my approach to my job?

4. Accomplishments:
- Within each job, did I merely list historically what I had done, or did I state my accomplishments with an eye to what would interest the reader in my target area?
- Are the accomplishments easy to read?
  - Bulleted rather than long paragraphs.
  - No extraneous words.
  - Action-oriented.
  - Measurable and specific.
  - Relevant. Would be of interest to the readers in my target area. Either the accomplishment is something they would want me to do for them, or it shows the breadth of my experience.

5. Overall Appearance:
- Is there plenty of white space? Or is the information squeezed so I can get it on one or two pages?
- Is it laid out nicely so it can serve as my marketing brochure?

6. Miscellaneous:
- Length: is the résumé as short as it can be while still being readable?
- Writing style: can the reader understand the point I am trying to make in each statement?
- Clarity: am I just hoping the reader will draw the right conclusion from what I've said? Or do I take the trouble to state things so clearly that there is no doubt that the reader will come away with the right message?
- Completeness: is all important information included? Have all dates been accounted for?
- Typos: is my résumé error-free?

PART SIX

WHAT IS THE FIVE O'CLOCK CLUB?

"AMERICA'S PREMIER CAREER COUNSELING NETWORK"

How to Join the Club

The Five O'Clock Club:

- Job-Search Strategy Groups
  - Private Coaching
- Membership Information

The Five O'Clock Club was founded by Kate Wendleton in 1978 to provide thoughtful career-development help for busy people of all levels. The programs and materials have helped thousands take control of their careers and find good jobs fast.

The original Five O'Clock Club was formed in Philadelphia in 1883. It was made up of the leaders of the day, who shared their experiences "in a spirit of fellowship and good humor."

There *is* a Five O'Clock Club near you!
For more information on becoming a member, please fill out the Membership Application Form in this book, sign up on our Website at: http://www.FiveOClockClub.com or call: 1-800-538-6645, ext. 600

Note: Counseling session fees are in addition to membership fees.

The median number of years men have been with their current employer fell between 1983 and 1996 for most ages, the Bureau of Labor Statistics reports: from 7.3 to 6.1 years for ages 35 to 44 and from 15.3 to 10.5 years for ages 55 to 64. But the overall median held at about four years on the job, as the work force aged. For women, the median tenure rose overall.
Albert Karr, *The Wall Street Journal*, February 11, 1997

The Five O'Clock Club Search Process

The Five O'Clock Club process, as outlined in Kate Wendleton's books, is a targeted, strategic approach to career development and job search. Five O'Clock Club members become proficient at skills which prove invaluable during their *entire working live*s.

We train our members to *manage their careers*, and always look ahead to their *next* job search. Research shows that an average worker spends only four years in a job—and will have 12 jobs, in as many as 5 career fields—during his or her working life.

Five O'Clock Club members find *better jobs, faster*. The average job search for a managerial position is now estimated at 8.1 months. The average Five O'Clock Club member who regularly attends weekly sessions finds a job by his or her tenth session. Even the discouraged, long-term job searcher can find immediate help.

The keystone to The Five O'Clock Club process is in teaching our members an understanding of the entire job-hiring process. A first interview is only a time for exchanging critical information. The real work starts after the interview. We teach our members *how to turn job interviews into offers*, and to negotiate the best possible employment package.

The Five O'Clock Club is *action-oriented*. **We'll help you decide what you should do this very next week to move your search along**. By their third session, our members have set definite job targets by industry or company size, position, and geographic location, and are out in the field, gathering information and making the contacts which will lead to interviews with hiring managers.

Our approach evolves with the changing job market. We're able to synthesize information from hundreds of Five O'Clock Club members, and come up with new approaches for our members. For example, we now discuss temporary placement for executives, how to handle voice mail, and how to network when doors are slamming shut all over town.

The Job-Search Strategy Group

The Five O'Clock Club meeting is a carefully planned *job-search strategy session*. We provide members with the tools and tricks necessary to get a good job fast—even in a tight market.Networking and emotional support are also included in the meeting.

Each week, you will **listen to a lecture** on some aspect of the Five O'Clock Club methodology. Then you will **join a small group strategy session** led by a trained Five O'Clock Club career consultant.

Hear one lecture per week via one of 16 audiotaped lectures by Kate Wendleton. (The boxed lecture set is $150 or comes FREE with the purchase of 10 Virtual Branch sessions.)

Join the *weekly small group strategy session* with a senior Five O'Clock Club career consultant via teleconference from the convenience of your home, or anywhere else. Your *small group* is your chance to get feedback and advice on your own search, listen to and learn from others, and build your business network. All groups are led by trained career consultants who bring years of experience to your search. The teleconferenced small group is generally no more than six people, so everyone gets the chance to speak up.

Members are urged to attend at least 10 meetings in a row to develop momentum and perhaps land an appropriate position. Our research proves that those who attend on a regular basis get jobs faster and at higher rates of pay than those who attend sporadically, search on their own or even those who see a coach privately throughout the process.

(optional) Virtual Branch members: Enjoy the Five O'Clock Club website and private message boards for your small group.

FEES: Our competitors charge $5000 to $7000 up front. The Five O'Clock Club costs less than ten percent of that! See our website for the counseling staff, the full offerings and the fees at the branch of your choice.

Private Coaching

Club Members: we will review your background and refer you to appropriate certified Five O'Clock Club career counselors. Fill out the Coach Request Form on FiveOClockClub.com, or meet with your group head between meetings for *private coaching*. Individual sessions help you answer specific questions, prepare your résumé, or take an in-depth look at your career path. Please pay the consultant directly, as *private coaching is <u>not</u> included in The Five O'Clock Club seminar or membership fee.*

From the Club history, written in the 1890s

At The Five O'Clock Club, [people] of all shades of political belief—as might be said of all trades and creeds—have met together. . . The variety continues almost to a monotony. . . [The Club's] good fellowship and geniality—not to say hospitality—has reached them all.

It has been remarked of clubs that they serve to level rank. If that were possible in this country, it would probably be true, if leveling rank means the appreciation of people of equal abilities as equals; but in The Five O'Clock Club it has been a most gratifying and noteworthy fact that no lines have ever been drawn save those which are essential to the honor and good name of any association. Strangers are invited by the club or by any members, [as gentlepeople], irrespective of aristocracy, plutocracy or occupation, and are so treated always. Nor does the thought of a [person's] social position ever enter into the meetings. People of wealth and people of moderate means sit side by side, finding in each other much to praise and admire and little to justify snarlishness or adverse criticism. People meet as people—not as the representatives of a set—and having so met, dwell not in worlds of envy or distrust, but in union and collegiality, forming kindly thoughts of each other in their heart of hearts.

In its methods, The Five O'Clock Club is plain, easy-going and unconventional. It has its "isms" and some peculiarities of procedure, but simplicity characterizes them all. The sense of propriety, rather than rules of order, governs its meetings, and that informality which carries with it sincerity of motive and spontaneity of effort, prevails within it. Its very name indicates informality, and, indeed, one of the reasons said to have induced its adoption was the fact that members or guests need not don their dress suits to attend the meetings, if they so desired. This informality, however, must be distinguished from the informality of Bohemianism. For The Five O'Clock Club, informality, above convenience, means sobriety, refinement of thought and speech, good breeding and good order. To this sort of informality much of its success is due.

Questions You May Have About the Weekly Job-Search Strategy Group

The Weekly Job-Search Strategy Group

is a Professional Career-Counseling Program presented at branches of The Five O'Clock Club.
"America's Premier Career Counseling Network"

Job hunters are not always the best judges of what they need during a search. For example, most are interested in lectures on answering ads or working with search firms. We will cover those topics, but, strategically, they are relatively unimportant in an effective job search.

At The Five O'Clock Club, you get the information you *really* need in your search—such as *how to target more effectively, how to get more interviews, and how to turn job interviews into offers.*

What's more, you will work in a small group with some of the best counselors available. In these strategy sessions, your group will help you decide what to do, this week and every week, to move your search along. And you will learn by coaching and being coached by others in your group.

Here are a few other points:

• For best results, attend on a regular basis. Your group gets to know you and will coach you to eliminate whatever you may be doing wrong—or refine what you are doing right.

• Those who think they need to come to a session only to ask a quick question are usually wrong. Often the problem started weeks before the job hunter realized it. Or the problem may be more complex than the job hunter realizes and requires a few sessions to straighten out.

• **You must be a member to attend the strategy sessions**. To get started in the small group sessions, you must purchase a minimum of 10 sessions, which *includes* the set of 16 audiotaped presentations on Five O'Clock Club methodology.

• After that, you may purchase five or ten sessions.

• **If you miss a session**, you may make it up at any time. You may even transfer unused sessions to a friend! (or use it during your next search).

• Carefully read all of the material in the Beginner's Kit that you get with your Five O'Clock Club membership. It will help you decide whether or not to attend.

• Although many people find jobs quickly (even people who have been unemployed a long time), others have more difficult searches. Plan to be in it for the long haul and you'll do better.

• The first week, pay attention to the strategies used by the others in your group. Soak up all the information you can. We will work on your search the *second* week.

• *Read the books and listen to the lecture before you come in the second week.* They will help you move your search along.

To register

1. For an application and pricing information, visit our website or call 1-800-538-6645 ext. 600.

2. Become a member and get your Beginner's Kit; then reserve a space by calling 212-286-9332.

3. You will get instructions on how to attend your first small-group teleconferencing session.

To assign you to a small group counselor, we need to know:

• your current (or last) field or industry,

• the kind of job you would like next (if you know),

• your desired salary range in general terms.

• your time zone/geographic location.

If you would rather see a private counselor, fill out the Coach Request Form on our website.

What Happens at the Meetings?

Each week, job searchers from various industries and professions attend. Some branches specialize in professionals and managers; others in those earning more than $100,00 per year; still others in recent college graduates, or those who have yet reached the professional or managerial ranks. Usually, half are employed; half unemployed.

Before the meeting, listen to the tape on a Five O'Clock Club job-hunting topic. Then, job hunters meet weekly in small groups headed by senior full-time, professional counselors.

The first week, you get the textbooks, listen to the lecture, are assigned to your small group, and *listen to the others in your group*. You learn a lot by listening to how your peers are strategizing their searches.

By the second week, you will have read the materials. Now we can start to work on your search

We find ourselves not independently of other people and institutions but through them.
We never get to the bottom of our selves on our own. We discover who we are face to face
and side by side with others in work, love, and learning.
Robert N. Bellah, et al, *Habits of the Heart*

strategy and help you decide what to do next to move your search along. For example, we'll help you figure out how to get more interviews in your target area, or how to turn an interview into a job offer.

In the third week, you will see major progress in the other members of your group, and you may notice major progress in your own search as well.

By the third or fourth week, most members are conducting a full and effective search. Over the remaining weeks, you will tend to keep up a full search rather than go after only one possibility. You will regularly aim to have six to ten things in the works at all times. These will generally be in specific target areas that you have identified, will keep your search on target, and increase your chances of getting multiple job offers to choose from.

Those who stick with the process find that it works.

Some people prefer to just observe for a few weeks before they start their job search, and that's okay, too.

How Much Does it Cost?

The fees vary by salary level and location. A typical fee is 10 sessions for $400 for those earning under $100,000 per year, and 10 sessions for $600 for those who have earned $100,000 and over. The average person purchases only 10 sessions, although those with difficult searches may need more time.

You must have the materials so you can review them before the second session. Otherwise, you will tend to waste the time of the others in the group by asking questions that are covered in the texts.

Is The Club right for me?

The Five O'Clock Club process is for you if:
- You are looking for a job or consulting work.
- You are a professional, manager or executive. (Most attendees earn between $30,000 and $300,000 a year, although some earn more and others earn less than those amounts.)
- You want to participate in a group process on a regular basis.
- You realize that finding or changing jobs and careers is hard work . . . which you are absolutely willing and able to do.

If you have no idea about the kind of job you want next, attend the first session, get the assessment assignment from your counselor, see the counselor privately for one or two sessions to develop tentative

job targets, and come back to the group with tentative targets in place. Since you don't participate the first week, it is usually best to join the group immediately and get your assignment. If you would prefer to see privately a counselor other than your group head, just fill out the "Coach Request Form" on our site.

How long will it take me to get a job?

Although our members tend to be from difficult fields or industries, the average person who attends regularly finds a new position within just ten sessions. Some take less time, and others take more. One thing we know for sure: *Those who get regular group coaching during their searches get jobs faster and at higher rates of pay than those who search on their own, simply take a course, or even those who choose to see a counselor privately throughout their searches.* This makes sense. If a person comes only when they think they have a problem, they are usually wrong. They probably had a problem a few weeks ago, but didn't realize it. Or the problem may be different from what they thought. Those who come regularly benefit from the observations others make about their searches. Problems are solved before they become severe, or are prevented altogether.

Those who attend regularly also learn a lot by paying attention and helping others in the group. This "vicarious" learning can cut weeks from your search. When you hear the problems of others who are ahead of you in the search, you can avoid those problems completely. People in your group will come to know you, and will point out subtleties you may not have noticed and interviewers will never tell you.

Will I be with others from my same field/industry?

Probably, but it's not that important. If you were a salesperson, for example, would you want to be with seven other salespeople?

Probably not. The search techniques are the same for the level handled by your branch. You will learn a lot and have a much more creative search if you are in a group with people who are in your general salary range but not exactly like you. Our clients are from virtually every field and industry. The process is what will help you. You will love the small group.

We've been doing this since 1978, and under-

The Five O'Clock Club is plain, easy-going and unconventional. . . .
Members or guests need not don their dress suits to attend the meetings.
(From the Club History, written in the 1890s)

stand your needs. That's why the mix we provide is the best you can get.

How can you charge such a small session fee?

1. We have no advertising costs because 90 percent of those who attend have been referred by other members.

We need a certain number of people to cover expenses. When lots of people get jobs quickly and leave us, we could go into the red. But so long as members refer others, we will continue to provide this service at a fair price.

2. We focus strictly on job search strategy, and encourage our clients to attend free support groups if they need emotional support. We focus on getting jobs, which reduces the time clients spend with us and the amount they pay.

3. We attract the best counselors, and our clients make more progress per session than they would elsewhere, which also reduces their costs.

4. We have expert administrators and a sophisticated computer system that reduces our overhead and increases our ability to track your progress.

May I change counselors?

Yes. Some care is taken in assigning you to your initial counselor. However, if you want to change once for any reason, you may do it. We don't encourage group hopping: It is better for you to stick with a group so that everyone gets to know you. On the other hand, we want you to feel comfortable. So if you tell us that you prefer a different group, you will be transferred immediately.

What if I have questions outside of the group?

Some people prefer to see their group counselor privately. Others prefer to meet with a different counselor to get another point of view. Whatever you decide, remember that the group fee does not cover counselor time outside of the group session. Therefore, if you want to be able to ask a counselor a "quick question" in between sessions, you would normally meet with the counselor first (usually by phone) for a private session so he or she gets to know you better. "Easy, quick questions" are often more complicated than they appear on the surface. After your first private session, some counselors will allow you to establish an account by paying in advance for one hour of counsel-ing time, which you can then use for quick questions (usually a 15-minute minimum is charged). Since each counselor has an individual way of operating, find out how the counselor arranges these things.

What if I want to start my own business?

The process of becoming a consultant is essentially the same as job hunting, and lots of consultants attend regular Five O'Clock Club meetings. However, if you want to buy a franchise or an existing business or start a growth business, you should see a private counselor who specializes in entrepreneurial counseling.

What if I'm still not sure what to do.

Members may sometimes be allowed to pay for a single session before signing up for the entire package.

Whatever you decide, just remember that it has been proven that those who receive regular small group help during their searches get a job faster and at higher rates of pay than those who search on their own or simply attend a course.

If you get a job just one or two weeks faster because of this program, it will more than have paid for itself. And you may transfer unused sessions to anyone you choose (who must become a member of the Club and pay for the remaining sessions).

What if I need help negotiating my severance or outplacement services?

If you are a professional, manager or executive and think you are about to lose your job, we can help you to negotiate your severance with your employer. *We have even helped consultants, part-timers and short-timers negotiate severance packages* well in excess of what they expected. **An outplacement firm cannot advise you** (since they are hired by your employer), but we can.

Just visit our website for helpful information -- including **letters you can actually hand to your employer**. In addition, we can assign you a career counselor to help in your negotiation -- for a modest hourly fee.

Fortune 500 as well as smaller **corporations and not-for-profits have paid for their employees to use The Five O'Clock Club's services**. Maybe you can get your employer to give you the same kind of help. Take a look at our website: **www.FiveOClockClub.com**.

The Five
O'Clock
Club®

The Way We Are

Just like the members of the original Five O'Clock Club, today's members want an ongoing relationship. George Vaillant, in his seminal work on successful people, found that "what makes or breaks our luck seems to be . . . our sustained relationships with other people." (George E. Vaillant, *Adaptation to Life*)

Five O'Clock Club members know that much of the program's benefit comes from simply showing up. Showing up will encourage you to do what you need to do when you are not here. And over the course of several weeks, certain things will become evident that are not evident now.

Five O'Clock Club members learn from each other: The group leader is not the only one with answers. The leader brings factual information to the meetings, and keeps the discussion in line. But the answers to some problems may lie within you, or with others in the group.

Five O'Clock Club members encourage each other. They listen, see similarities with their own situations, and learn from that. And they listen to see how they may help others. You may come across information or a contact that will help someone else in the group. Passing on that information is what we're all about.

If you are a new member here, listen to others to learn the process. And read the books so you will know the basics that others already know. When everyone understands the basics, this keeps the meetings on a high level, interesting, and helpful to everyone.

Five O'Clock Club members are in this together, but they know that ultimately they are each responsible for solving their own problems with God's help. Take the time to learn the process, and you will become better at analyzing your own situation, as well as the situations of others. You will be learning a method that will serve you the rest of your life, and in areas of your life apart from your career.

Five O'Clock Club members are kind to each other. They control their frustrations—because venting helps no one. Because many may be stressed, be kind and go the extra length to keep this place calm and happy. It is your respite from the world outside and a place for you to find comfort and FUN. Relax and enjoy yourself, learn what you can, and help where you can. And have a ball doing it.

Use The Five O'Clock Club lexicon as a shorthand to express where you are in your job search. It will focus you and those in your group.

I. Overview and Assessment

How many hours a week are you spending on your search? Spend 35 hours on a full-time search; 15 hours on a part-time search.

What are your job targets?
  Tell the group. A target includes industry or company size, position, and geographic area.
  The group can help assess how good your targets are. Take a look at "Measuring Your Targets."

How does your résumé position you?
The summary and body should make you look appropriate to your target.

What are your back-up targets?
Decide at the beginning of the search before the first campaign. Then you won't get stuck.

Have you done the Assessment? If your targets are wrong, everything is wrong. (Do the Assessment in *Targeting the Job You Want.*) Or a counselor can help you privately to determine possible job targets.

II. Getting Interviews

How large is your target (e.g., thirty companies)? How many of them have you contacted? Contact them all.

How can you get (more) leads?
You will not get a job through search firms, ads, networking or direct contact. Those are techniques for getting interviews—job leads. Use the right terminology, especially after a person gets a job. Do not say, "How did you get the job?" if you really want to know, "Where did you get the lead for that job?"

Do you have six to ten things in the works?
You may want the group to help you land one job. After they help you with your strategy, they should ask, "How many other things do you have in the works?" If "none," the group can brainstorm how you can get more things going: through search firms, ads, networking, or direct contact. Then you are more likely to turn the interview into an offer because you will seem more valuable. What's more,

five will fall away through no fault of your own. Don't go after only one job.

How's your Two-Minute Pitch?
Practice a *tailored* Two-Minute Pitch. Tell the group the job title and industry of the hiring manager they should pretend they are for a role-playing exercise.
  You will be surprised how good the group is at critiquing pitches. (Practice a few weeks in a row.) Use your pitch to separate you from your competition.

You seem to be in Stage One (or Stage Two or Stage Three) of your search. Know where you are. This is the key measure of your search.

Are you seen as insider or outsider?
See "How to Change Careers" for becoming an insider. If people are saying, "I wish I had an opening for someone like you," you are doing well in meetings. If the industry is strong, then it's only a matter of time before you get a job.

III. Turning Interviews into Offers

Do you want this job?
If you do not want the job, perhaps you want an offer, if only for practice. If you are not willing to go for it, the group's suggestions will not work.

Who are your likely competitors and how can you outshine and outlast them? You will not get a job simply because "they liked me." The issues are deeper. Ask the interviewer: "Where are you in the hiring process? What kind of person would be your ideal candidate? How do I stack up?"

What are your next steps? What are *you* planning to do if the hiring manager doesn't call by a certain date, or what are you planning to do to assure that the hiring manager *does* call you?

Can you prove you can do the job? Don't just take the "Trust me" approach. Consider your competition.

Which job positions you best for the long run? Which job is the best fit? Don't decide only on the basis of salary. You will most likely have another job after this. See which job looks best on your résumé, and will make you stronger for the next time.
  In addition, find a fit for your personality. If you don't "fit," it is unlikely you will do well there. The group can help you turn interviews into offers, and give you feedback on which job is best for you.

The Five O'Clock Club®

Dear Prospective Five O'Clock Clubber:

The Five O'Clock Club has helped thousands find jobs, change, or manage their careers!

At The Five O'Clock Club, we focus your search with real-world information that tells you exactly what you need to get more interviews . . . **and turn those interviews into offers.**

As a member, you also get—

❑ An attractive **membership card** and a **Beginner's Kit** containing information based on 12 years of research regarding who gets jobs and why, that will enable you to improve your job-search technqiues . . . immediately.

❑ A **subscription to *The Five O'Clock News***, ten issues filled with information on career development and job-search techniques— information to help you thrive in your career.

❑ **Access to reasonably priced weekly seminars** featuring individualized attention to your specific needs in small groups supervised by our senior counselors.

❑ Access to **one-on-one counselor matching**.

❑ Access to **members-only Bulletin Boards** to exchange ideas, experiences, and even role-play with other job searchers and career changers.

All that access, all that information, for the nominal membership fee of only $49.

The sooner you become a member, the sooner you can begin working on having a career that truly meets your financial, emotional, creative and intellectual needs.

Believe me, with self-examination and a lot of hard work with our counselors, you **can** find the job . . . you **can** have the career . . . you **can** live the life you always wanted!

The best of luck, whatever you may decide.

Sincerely,
Kate Wendleton, President

❑ Yes! I want access to the most effective methods for developing and managing my career, as well as for finding jobs.

. . . .

I enclose ❑ $49.00 for one year ❑ $75.00 for two years.
(foreign membership: $59 for one year; $85.00 for two)
I will receive ✓ a Beginner's Kit, ✓ a membership card, ✓ a subscription to *The Five O'Clock News*, ✓ a listing of current branches of The Five O'Clock Club, ✓ access to a network of career counselors (fees vary); ✓ to reasonably priced seminars at branches of The Five O'Clock Club in the U.S. and Canada; and ✓ to the members-only section of www.FiveOClockClub.com. ✓ other benefits listed on our website: www.FiveOClockClub.com.

Name _____

Address _____

City _____ State/Prov. _____ Zip/Postal _____

Work Phone _____ Home _____

Email address _____

Today's Date: _____

How I heard about you: _____

Building a Great Resume
. . . .

Method of payment:

❑ I enclose my check made out to The Five O'Clock Club, 300 E. 40th St., Suite 6L, NY, NY 10016.
❑ MasterCard, VISA or American Express:
(This form can be faxed to 212-286-9571)

Account Number: _____

Exp. Date: _____ Signature: _____

. . . .

The following information is for statistical purposes. Thanks for your help.

Salary range:

❑ under $30,000   ❑ $30-$49,999   ❑ $50-$74,999
❑ $75-$99,999   ❑ $100-$125,000   ❑ over $125,000

Age: ❑ 20-29   ❑ 30-39   ❑ 40-49   ❑ 50+

Gender: ❑ Male   ❑ Female

Current or most recent position/title: _____

_____

. . . .

The original Five O'Clock Club® was formed in Philadelphia in 1883. It was made up of the leaders of the day, who shared their experiences "in a spirit of fellowship and good humor."

Index

About the Author

Kate Wendleton is a nationally syndicated careers columnist and recognized authority on career development, having appeared on the *Today* Show, CNN, CNBC, Larry King, National Public Radio and CBS, and in *The New York Times*, *The Chicago Tribune*, *The Wall Street Journal*, *Fortune* magazine, *Business Week* and other national media.

She has been a career coach since 1978, when she founded The Five O'Clock Club® and developed its methodology to help job hunters and career changers of all levels in job-search-strategy groups. This methodology is now used by Affiliates of The Five O'Clock Club, which meet weekly in the United States and Canada.

Kate also founded Workforce America®, a not-for-profit Affiliate of The Five O'Clock Club, serving adults in Harlem who are not yet in the professional or managerial ranks. Workforce America helps each person move into better-paying, higher-level positions as each improves in educational level and work experience.

Kate founded, and directed for seven years, The Career Center at The New School for Social Research in New York. She also advises major corporations about employee career-development programs, and coaches senior executives.

A former CFO of two small companies, she has twenty years of business-management experience in both manufacturing and service businesses.

Kate attended Chestnut Hill College in Philadelphia and received her MBA from Drexel University. She is a popular speaker with groups that include the Wharton Business School Club, the Yale Club and the Columbia Business School Club.

While living in Philadelphia, Kate did long-term volunteer work for the Philadelphia Museum of Art, the Walnut Street Theatre Art Gallery, United Way, and the YMCA. Kate currently lives in Manhattan.

Kate Wendleton is the author of The Five O'Clock Club's four-part career-development and job-hunting series: *Targeting the Job You Want*, *Getting Interviews*, *Interviewing and Salary Negotiation* and *Building a Great Résumé*.

The original Five O'Clock Club was formed in Philadelphia in 1883.
It was made up of the leaders of the day, who shared their experiences
"in a spirit of fellowship and good humor."